Series authors:
Malcolm Mann
Steve Taylore-Knowles

Laser A1+

Workbook with key

MACMILLAN

Macmillan Education
4 Crinan Street
London N1 9XW
A division of Macmillan Publishers Limited
Companies and representatives throughout the world

ISBN 978-0-230-42463-0 (with Answer key)
978-0-230-42464-7 (without Answer key)
978-0-230-42461-6 (with Answer key plus Audio CD)
978-0-230-42462-3 (without Answer key plus Audio CD)

Series authors: Malcolm Mann & Steve Taylore-Knowles

First published 2012

Original design by Peter Burgess
Page make-up by Red Giraffe
Illustrated by Ilias Arahovitis pp7, 20, 25, 40, 49, 76;
Red Giraffe pp21, 36, 48, 52, 64, 93;
Alek Sotirovski pp17, 19, 27, 65, 85
Cover design by Peter Burgess
Picture research by Susannah Jayes

The authors and publishers would like to thank the following for permission to reproduce their photographs:

Alamy/Cultura Creative p56, Alamy/Jason Gallier p54, Alamy/Photo Network p12, Alamy/Purestock p28, Alamy/Vika Sabo p35, Alamy/Philip Scalia p87, Alamy/Dave Stamboulis p4, Alamy/David Young-Wolff p30; **Corbis** p38, Corbis/Atlantide Phototravel p17, Corbis/Ocean p6, Corbis/Mark Peterson p45; **Getty Images**/Camelot p27, Getty Images/Comstock p33, Getty Images/Ned Frisk p15, Getty Images/Thinkstock p57.

Printed and bound in Thailand

2017 2016 2015 2014
10 9 8 7 6 5

Contents

1

This is Me!

Reading

1 **Read the personal profiles and for each question, choose the correct answer, A, B or C.**

My name is Seamus, and I'm from London, England. I'm thirteen years old. I haven't got any brothers or sisters but I have a lot of cousins on my mother's side. My grandparents – my mum's mother and father – have a large house in the country. It's very noisy when my cousins and I are all there visiting. My best friend's name is Bridgit. We love playing computer games and watching TV together.
Seamus, England

Hello. I'm Aini. I'm from Cairo, Egypt and my family is very big – and very close. We all love each other very much. I've got three brothers and a sister. We've got a big house and I share a room with my sister. Her name is Izza and she is my best friend. We do a lot of things together: read, listen to music and draw. My father doesn't like cats or dogs, so we don't have a pet. Izza and I want to travel to lots of places and see the world!
Aini, Egypt

Hi, my name's Bach and I'm from a small town in Poland. I am twelve years old and I'm in Year 9 at school. I have two sisters. They are called Anastasia and Katerina. I don't like spending time with them – they are very noisy! I've got lots of friends but my best friend is Anetta. She's great. I have a dog and Anetta has a dog. We love walking our dogs in the country. Anetta and I want to travel to America and visit the people we chat with online.
Bach, Poland

1 Seamus is an only child.
A Right **B** Wrong **C** Doesn't say

2 Seamus spends a lot of time at his grandparents' house.
A Right **B** Wrong **C** Doesn't say

3 Aini has her own room.
A Right **B** Wrong **C** Doesn't say

4 There are five children in Aini's family.
A Right **B** Wrong **C** Doesn't say

5 Bach and Anetta have got pets.
A Right **B** Wrong **C** Doesn't say

6 Bach's school is Anetta's school.
A Right **B** Wrong **C** Doesn't say

Wordpower!

2 **Match the words and phrases with their definitions (a–f).**

1 best friend ___
2 the country ___
3 share ___
4 chat online ___
5 an only child ___
6 close friend ___

a not your favourite friend but a person you love a lot
b a person that hasn't got a brother or sister
c when you do this, it means you use something (eg a room) with another person
d when you talk to people using a computer and the internet
e a place with trees, outside a city
f the friend you love best

3 **Choose the correct word or phrase.**

www.ivanblog.co.uk

Hello!
My name is Ivan and I'm from Poland. My parents and I live in a large house in the (1) **friend / country** – it's very nice. I'm a(n) (2) **only child / close friend**, so I haven't got any brothers or sisters. I've got lots of friends, so I don't get lonely. My (3) **close / best** friend in the world is Albin and I (4) **chat / share** everything with him – my computer, my TV and my games. I've got other (5) **best / close** friends at school too. Let's be friends and we can (6) **share / chat** online. Do you want to do that and we can tell each other about our lives?
Write soon!
Ivan

Grammar 1

be, have/have got

Look again at *Grammar database 1* on page 145 before doing these exercises.

1 **Tick (✔) the correct sentences.**

1 Has he got a brother? ☐
2 We're not American. ☐
3 No, it haven't. ☐
4 I hasn't got a big house. ☐
5 Does he have a computer? ☐
6 She doesn't has a best friend. ☐
7 Bach is from Poland. ☐
8 You has lots of close friends. ☐

2 Complete the text with one word for each gap.

My name (1) ________ Falah and I am from Cairo. I (2) ________ twelve years old. I (3) ________ a brother and a sister but I haven't (4) ________ a dog or a cat. (5) ________ you have a pet? I don't have a lot of friends but I (6) ________ got two very close ones. Their names (7) ________ Asad and Badr. We spend a lot of time playing computer games and watching TV. (8) ________ you got a best friend? Maybe I can be your best friend!

3 Answer the questions using short answers.

1 Are we friends? No, ________.
2 Does Petros have a close friend? Yes, ________.
3 Has she got a cat? Yes, ________.
4 Do you have a sister? No, ________.
5 Has it got a name? No, ________.
6 Are they lonely? Yes, ________.

4 Rewrite the sentences using the words in bold.

1 Has he got a brother? **does** *Does he have a brother?*
2 Beth and Marge haven't got a TV. **don't** ________
3 Have you got a large house? **do** ________
4 My cat hasn't got a name. **have** ________
5 He doesn't have a computer. **got** ________
6 I don't have a lot of friends. **got** ________
7 Does Sophia have a best friend? **has** ________
8 Do they have a pet? **got** ________

Wordpower!

1 Write a word in each gap to complete the sentences. The first letter is given to help you.

1 My **g**__________, Tom, is married to my great-grandmother, Ruth.
2 I often play with my **n**__________. He's my sister's son.
3 My dad's father, my **g**__________, is ninety years old.
4 Has your **u**__________, your mum's brother, got a nice house?
5 My brother's daughter is my **n**__________.
6 These are my **c**__________, George and Emily. They are my Aunt Beth's children.
7 Her **g**__________, her mum's mother, is from England.
8 I am an only child. I don't have a **b**__________ or a sister.
9 Does your **g**__________, your father's grandmother, live with you?
10 Bryda's **a**__________ is her father's sister.

2 For each question, choose the correct answer, A or B.

1 My brother has one daughter. She's my ___.
A aunt **B** niece

2 His ___, his mother's grandfather, hasn't got hair.
A great-grandfather **B** nephew

3 Do your great-grandfather and your ___ have a lot of children?
A uncle **B** great-grandmother

4 Izzy's sister has got one son. He is Izzy's ___.
A grandfather **B** nephew

5 Do you spend a lot of time with your mother's mum, your ___?
A grandmother **B** brother

6 Bach's ___, his mum's dad, has a lot of pets.
A sister **B** grandfather

7 Martha's ___, her aunt's son, is in Year 5.
A cousin **B** great-grandfather

8 Her ___, her father's sister, lives in the country.
A aunt **B** niece

9 My ___ is married to my Aunt Edna.
A uncle **B** great-grandmother

10 Have you got a ___ or a sister? Or are you an only child?
A grandmother **B** brother

Listening

CD Track 1

1 Listen to three people talking about their friends and family. Match the speakers with the statements (a–d). There is one letter you do not need to use.

1 Speaker 1: ___
2 Speaker 2: ___
3 Speaker 3: ___

a has a large family
b is an only child
c hasn't got a pet
d lives in the country

CD Track 1

2 Listen again and underline the words you hear.

1 Manu is **eight / thirteen** years old.
2 Manu's **father / brother** is called Wafi.
3 Eileen has got three **sisters / cousins**.
4 Eileen's best friend is **Jo-Jo / Sheila**.
5 Miguel has two **friends / dogs**.

Grammar 2

G

Possessives

Look again at *Grammar database 2* on page 146 before doing these exercises.

1 Write a word in each gap to complete the sentences.

1 That's ____________ ! See, it's got ____________ name on it.
my mine
2 Those cats are ____________ and that is ____________ dog too.
their theirs
3 Pam and Bach are ____________ cousins. That house is ____________ .
hers her
4 Giselle, that's not ____________ laptop. It's ____________ .
your ours
5 Is that ____________ dog? What's ____________ name?
its your
6 This is ____________ bike. Where's ____________ ?
yours his

2 Complete the table.

	Possessive adjective	Possessive pronoun
I	(1)	mine
you	your	(2)
he	his	(3)
she	(4)	hers
it	(5)	its
we	our	(6)
they	(7)	(8)

3 **Read the text and for each question, choose the correct answer, A, B or C.**

Dear Phillipa,
(1) ___ name is Petra and I am from Germany. I have got a big family. I have got two brothers and one sister. My (2) ___ names are Franz and Fritz – (3) ___ are twins. My (4) ___ name is Anne. My family has got a large house. It's got four bedrooms. My sister and I have got (5) ___ own rooms but my brothers share a room. (6) ___ room is always very noisy ... not like (7) ___! We have a big dog. (8) ___ name is Wolf. It hasn't got its own room! It spends a lot of time in the (9) ___ room. Please write and tell me about (10) ___ family.
Bye for now,
Petra

	A	B	C
1	**A** Mine	**B** My	**C** I
2	**A** brothers'	**B** brothers	**C** brother's
3	**A** their	**B** theirs	**C** they
4	**A** sisters	**B** sister's	**C** sisters'
5	**A** our	**B** ours	**C** we
6	**A** They	**B** Their	**C** Theirs
7	**A** my	**B** mine	**C** I
8	**A** It's	**B** Its	**C** It
9	**A** twins	**B** twin's	**C** twins'
10	**A** you	**B** your	**C** yours

✔ Quick check

4 **Choose the correct answer.**

1 Do we use *be* to describe what things and people are like? **yes / no**
2 Do we use *have* to talk about what things and people possess? **yes / no**
3 Do *have got* and *have* mean something different? **yes / no**
4 Which one is correct? My sister **is / are** my best friend.
5 Which one is correct? **Do you have a cat? / Have you got a cat? / both**
6 Possessive adjectives come **before / after** a noun.
7 *My*, *your*, *her*, *our*, and *their* are possessive **adjectives / pronouns**.
8 After a plural noun ending in *–s*, we put the apostrophe **before / after the 's'**.

Writing

1 **Rewrite the sentences using short forms.**

1 I am Zak and I am twelve years old. ______________________
2 I am quite tall and I have got brown hair. ______________________
3 My cousin has got blue eyes. ______________________
4 She does not have many friends. ______________________
5 No, I do not. ______________________
6 This is my favourite book – it is full of funny stories. ______________________

2

On the Farm!

Reading

1 Read the texts and for each question, choose the correct answer, A, B or C.

I love living on a farm. My day starts very early. I wake up at a quarter to five, I get ready and then I start my work. First I give the animals their food then I milk the cows. After that, I visit the chickens to collect the eggs. I'm back at the house at half past eight. I have breakfast and do some work in the house, then I sleep for an hour after lunch. That's my favourite time of the day, I think!

1 This person …

A likes to sleep in the afternoon.

B doesn't like farm life.

C only does two different jobs.

I love it when children come to the farm. They have a great time with the animals! We've got many different kinds. We've got horses, goats, ducks, sheep, ponies, cows and calves. The children love to stroke the ponies and watch the calves. But the great thing about having children on the farm is that they learn how farms work. That's what I really love!

2 This person …

A hasn't got baby animals on the farm.

B has got chickens on the farm.

C likes children to learn about the farm.

I live in the city and I like it, but I really like visiting farms. Life there is very nice. It's very noisy in the city, so it's great to go to a farm and hear only the sounds of animals. My favourite sound is the sound of ducks. They make very funny noises! I also like the sounds that horses and cows make. You don't hear these sounds in the city at all, only cars and people. It's nice to hear something different for a change!

3 This person …

A doesn't like city life at all.

B thinks horses make funny noises.

C likes the sounds that ducks make.

My friend Ted lives on a farm. I go there at the weekends to have lunch sometimes. His mum cooks great food. She uses the fruit and vegetables that they've grown on their farm. After we have lunch, we ride the horses in the fields. That's my favourite thing to do. Ted's got three really nice horses. They're good fun to ride. It's nice to live on a farm like that!

4 This person …

A lives on a farm.

B has got a horse.

C likes to ride horses.

My family and I live in a small town and there are many farms around us. They've got different animals on the farms. One farm has got many cows so they sell milk. Another farm has got lots of chickens so they sell eggs. My mum and dad go to these farms to get milk and eggs because they're really good. I'm glad I don't live on a farm because it's a lot of work, but it's nice to live close to them!

5 This person …

A visits farms in his town.

B likes food from farms.

C thinks farm life is easy.

Wordpower!

2 Choose the correct word.

1 Do you **feed / pick** the animals every morning?
2 We **pick / plant** fruit from the trees in the afternoon.
3 Mrs Collins **strokes / plants** flowers in the spring.
4 Caroline likes to **welcome / touch** the ponies.
5 The farm workers **welcome / collect** children to the farm.
6 Everyone loves to **stroke / pick** the horses.
7 Mr Collins **plants / collects** eggs from the chickens.
8 Sally **picks / moves** the lambs to different places on the farm.

3 Read the text and for each question, choose the correct answer, A, B or C.

I live with my family on a farm, and we love it. My sister and I do many things to help. In the morning, we go and (1) ___ all the animals with Dad. They often eat all the food! Then we (2) ___ eggs from the chickens and we (3) ___ the sheep to different fields.

My sister likes (4) ___ the horses, and they like it too! I like the baby chicks and I really like (5) ___ them. They're very soft! After school in the afternoon, we help Mum with some things. My sister and my mum sometimes (6) ___ things in the ground in our garden.

I usually (7) ___ fruit from the trees and vegetables from the garden. Sometimes, people come to visit the farm, and I (8) ___ them and show them the animals.

	A	B	C
1	**A** pick	**B** feed	**C** plant
2	**A** collect	**B** touch	**C** welcome
3	**A** feed	**B** plant	**C** move
4	**A** stroking	**B** collecting	**C** planting
5	**A** picking	**B** welcoming	**C** touching
6	**A** pick	**B** plant	**C** feed
7	**A** plant	**B** move	**C** pick
8	**A** collect	**B** move	**C** welcome

Grammar 1 G

Present simple

Look again at *Grammar database 3* on page 146 before doing these exercises.

1 Write the verbs in the present simple.

1 My mum and dad ______________ (**work**) in the fields every day.
2 Joe ______________ (**not live**) in the city because it's not nice.
3 ______________ (**you/want**) to come and play with the animals?
4 Maddie ______________ (**go**) for rides on the donkey in the afternoon.
5 ______________ (**Ned/like**) to eat fruit and vegetables?
6 They ______________ (**not wake up**) very early in the morning.
7 My sister and I ______________ (**get up**) at 7 o'clock to help on the farm.
8 ______________ (**they/visit**) the city at the weekend?

2 Write sentences or questions using the present simple.

1 Visitors / leave / the farm / in the evening ____________________
2 Lisa / play / with the puppies / every day ____________________
3 Sally and I / not work / a lot / on the farm ____________________
4 your day / start / at 7am? ____________________
5 I / love / Ned the donkey ____________________
6 Peter and Joe / live / on the farm / all year? ____________________
7 The children / see / the calves in the afternoon ____________________
8 She / not eat / eggs for breakfast ____________________

3 Each of the words or phrases in bold is incorrect. Write the correct words on the lines.

1 Michelle **don't** know what farm life is like. __________
2 **Students do** learn how to collect eggs? __________
3 People **arrives** at 7 o'clock in the morning. __________
4 **Do** Paul move the horses to different fields? __________
5 He **take** the goats for a walk at noon. __________
6 Children **doesn't** ride the cows! __________
7 **Does** donkeys do a lot of work on the farm? __________
8 I **doesn't** stroke the ponies every day. __________

4 Choose the correct word.

My friend Paul (1) **live / lives** on a farm. I really (2) **likes / like** visiting him there. He and I (3) **feed / feeds** the animals when I (4) **visits / visit**. It's fun! The ponies and lambs (5) **play / plays** with us sometimes. They're really nice! There are some things Paul and I (6) **don't / doesn't** like doing. Paul (7) **don't / doesn't** like collecting eggs. I don't (8) **go / goes** near the horses. They (9) **runs / run** a lot and I (10) **don't / doesn't** like that! But everything else is great. Farms are a lot of fun!

Wordpower!

1 Write a word from the box in each gap.

hours • minutes • o'clock • past • quarter • seconds • watch

1 There are 60 ________ in one hour.
2 To say that it's thirty minutes after four o'clock, you say half ________ four.
3 There are 24 ________ in one day.
4 There are 60 ________ in a minute.
5 One hour after two o'clock is three ________ .
6 Fifteen minutes before five o'clock is a ________ to five.
7 A ________ is like a small clock and it gives you the time.

2 Choose the correct word or phrase.

I've got work to do on the farm every morning. My day starts at six (1) **o'clock / hour**. I get ready and at (2) **half / minute** past six, I go and feed the animals. It takes about (3) **an hour / a second** to give the cows all their food, sometimes more. Then, at quarter (4) **to / from** eight, I collect the eggs from the chickens. That only takes about 15 (5) **o'clock / minutes**. I stroke the horses for a few (6) **seconds / hours** and then, I'm finished! I look at my (7) **watch / hour.** It's eight o'clock– time for breakfast!

Listening

CD Track 2

1 Listen to two people talking on the phone and for each question, choose the correct answer, A or B.

1 Who is the woman on the phone?
A a teacher
B a farm worker

2 What does the man want to visit?
A a farm
B a town

3 When does the man want to visit?
A during the week
B at the weekend

CD Track 2

2 Listen again and complete the gaps.

Weekend Farm Trip

Name of farm:	Chester Farms
Town:	(1)
Opens at:	(2)
Animals:	cows, horses and (3)
Lunch time:	(4)
Closes at:	(5)

Grammar 2

Adverbs of frequency

Look again at *Grammar database 4* on page 146 before doing these exercises.

1 Write sentences using the present simple and the word or phrase in bold.

1 The Collins / visit / the city. **every week** ______________________
2 Frank / be / tired / at the end of the day. **usually** ______________________
3 you / ride / horses? **every day** ______________________
4 Susan / be / late / to feed the animals. **never** ______________________
5 Dad / get up / at five o'clock? **always** ______________________
6 I / be / busy / in the mornings. **often** ______________________

2 Tick (✔) the correct sentences. Underline the mistakes in the incorrect sentences and write the sentences correctly.

1 I wake up early in the morning never. ___ ______________________
2 We pick every year vegetables at this time. ___ ______________________
3 I usually sleep for 8 hours at night. ___ ______________________
4 The cows eat often all of their food. ___ ______________________
5 Mary arrives late always to the farm. ___ ______________________
6 Mum cooks every day lunch for us. ___ ______________________

3 Read the text and for each question, choose the correct answer, A, B or C.

I work on a farm and it is hard (1) ___ . I get up at six o'clock in the morning (2) ___ . I (3) ___ tired in the morning, but I (4) ___ wake up late. The animals (5) ___ their food! I (6) ___ them at seven o'clock, maybe a quarter past seven. They (7) ___ happy to see me! After I feed them, I (8) ___ the cows, or I collect the eggs, or I walk the horses. There (9) ___ a different job to do on the farm (10) ___ . That's one thing I love about it!

	A	B	C
1	**A** always	**B** often	**C** sometimes
2	**A** usually	**B** every day	**C** always
3	**A** often am	**B** am often	**C** sometimes am
4	**A** always	**B** usually	**C** never
5	**A** want always	**B** always want	**C** always wants
6	**A** usually feed	**B** feed usually	**C** usually feeds
7	**A** is always	**B** always are	**C** are always
8	**A** sometimes milks	**B** milk sometimes	**C** sometimes milk
9	**A** is usually	**B** usually are	**C** usually is
10	**A** often	**B** usually	**C** every week

Quick check

4 Choose the correct answer.

1 Do we use the present simple to talk about situations that always happen? **yes / no**
2 Which is correct? **They lives on a farm. / They live on a farm. / both**
3 Which is correct? **Does Sam feed the cows? / Do Sam feed the cows? / both**
4 Do we use adverbs of frequency to show when something happens? **yes / no**
5 Which is correct? **My dog is often happy. / My dog often is happy. / both**
6 Which is correct? **Ned sometimes runs. / Ned runs sometimes. / both**

Writing

1 Rewrite the sentences using *then* or *after*, as in the example.

1 We feed the animals. We collect eggs.
We feed the animals. Then we collect eggs. *After we feed the animals, we collect eggs.*
2 We wake up at seven. We help our dad with work. **then** __________
3 We have breakfast. We pick fruit and vegetables. **after** __________
4 We have lunch at one. We ride horses. **then** __________
5 We walk the ponies. We go home. **after** __________

2 Read the email and match each paragraph or part with a statement.

write reply send

A To: Lisa Kline <lkline@fastmail.com>
Subject: My farm visit!

B Hi, Lisa!

C How are you? I hope you're doing well. How are things in London?

D I'm at my friend Roger's farm. It's a lot of fun! We wake up at a quarter to seven every day and help Roger's dad feed the animals. Then we collect eggs and Roger's dad milks the cows. There are lots of other animals here – sheep, goats, ducks, two sheep dogs and many cats!

E After we feed the animals, we go back to the house. Roger's mum cooks breakfast. That's at half past eight. Then we go with Roger's mum to pick fruit and vegetables.

F We have lunch at half past one. Then we sometimes ride the horses or we take the dogs for a walk. It's great!

G Hope to talk to you soon!
Love,
Angela

1 This part says goodbye to Angela's friend. ___
2 This paragraph asks how Angela's friend is. ___
3 This part has got the email address. ___
4 This paragraph talks about Angela and Roger's first meal of the day. ___
5 This paragraph talks about what Angela and Roger do after lunch. ___
6 This paragraph says what Angela does with the animals in the morning. ___
7 This part says hello to Angela's friend. ___

Check your progress! | Units 1-2

1 Rewrite the words to complete the gaps in the text.

Our Family Farm

My name is Sam and I live on a farm in the (1) __________ (**oucrytn**). I've got a big family. I have two sisters, Bella and Helen, two brothers, Grant and Tom and lots of (2) __________ (**ounicss**). My (3) __________ (**dngrarethom**) and grandfather live in our house too. Life on a farm isn't a lazy life. The day starts early. Every day my family and I (4) __________ (**dfee**) all the animals, milk the cows and (5) __________ (**ltcelco**) the chickens' eggs, (6) __________ (**anlpt**) and pick fruit and vegetables, and do lots of other jobs. Of course, I don't work all the time. I've also got lots of time to spend with my (7) __________ (**tbse**) friend, Maggie.

7 marks

2 Put a line through the incorrect sentence.

8 I have two close friends. / I has two close friends.
9 My cousin is in the girls's room. / My cousin is in the girls' room.
10 Do Sheila feed the animals every day? / Does Sheila feed the animals every day?
11 Is you an only child? / Are you an only child?
12 Is your mother often late? / Is your mother late often?
13 Where's Peters' niece? / Where's Peter's niece?
14 They never go to the city. / They go to the city never.
15 They don't live in the country. / They doesn't live in the country.

8 marks

3 Put the words into the correct order to make sentences or questions.

16 vegetables? / plant / Do / fruit / you / and
____

17 hasn't / a / got / best / He / friend.
____

18 her / Look / in / bedroom.
____

19 and / Have / dog? / Sasha / got / Wendy / a
____

20 love / the / visiting / They / farm.
____

21 pony / mine. / is / That
____

22 Bob / every / has / day. / lunch
____

23 the / its / kitten / dinner. / Give
____

24 tired? / your / often / grandfather / Is
____

25 the morning. / brush / We / ponies / the / in / don't
____

10 marks

Total:____ **/ 25 marks**

3

Going Shopping!

Reading

1 Read the dialogues about shopping. Match the dialogues with the shops (a–d). There is one letter you do not need to use.

Dialogue 1

Girl: Excuse me. I wonder if you can help me. I'm looking for something special for my cousin. It's his birthday next Friday.

Man: Of course. We've got some lovely things for children.

Girl: He's seven years old and he loves books, and he loves animals. Well, he doesn't like cats.

Man: We haven't got books here but we've got some very nice things.

Girl: Oh, those are lovely!

Man: What? What are you looking at?

Girl: Those funny puppies! I love the red one. Oh, and the blue one! My cousin collects those animals. Are they expensive?

Dialogue 2

Boy: I'm getting hungry, Jane. Let's find somewhere to eat. It's half past two.

Girl: It's not half past two, Bob, it's only two. Let's go over there and look at those socks.

Boy: Socks! I don't want to look at socks! I'm feeling tired. This shop is busy and noisy and I'm not enjoying myself!

Girl: OK, let's sit down and rest on this bench. Oh, wait! Look! Lovely skirts! They're having a sale. Where are you going, Bob?

Boy: I want to look at the skirts.

Girl: No, you don't! You're going to the lift – there's a *Chicken World* on the second floor!

Dialogue 3

Woman: Can I help you?

Girl: Yes, please. I'm looking for some good ideas for my mum's birthday. It's today.

Woman: I understand. Does she like flowers?

Girl: Oh, yes. But I don't have a lot of money.

Woman: That's OK. We're doing a special offer at the moment. These aren't expensive.

Girl: Oh, they're lovely!

Woman: Great. Do you want the red ones?

Girl: Yes, please – twelve red ones.

1 Dialogue 1: ___
2 Dialogue 2: ___
3 Dialogue 3: ___

a bookshop
b toy shop
c clothes shop
d florist's

2 Read the dialogues again and answer the questions.

Dialogue 1:

1 Who is the girl buying a present for? ___________

2 What is the girl looking at? ___________

Dialogue 2:

3 How is the boy feeling? ___________

4 What doesn't the boy want to look at? ___________

Dialogue 3:

5 Who is having their birthday today? ___________

6 What does the girl's mother like? ___________

Wordpower!

3 **Complete the conversations. For each question, choose the correct answer, A, B or C.**

1 Let's go to the second floor.
A OK, but I want to take the lift.
B Oh, I love this skirt.
C I'm getting hungry.

2 Are you having fun shopping?
A Yes, I'm so busy.
B No, I'm happy.
C Yes, I'm enjoying myself!

3 The shop is very noisy, isn't it?
A Yes, shall we take the escalator?
B Yes, and also very busy!
C No, I'm getting bored.

4 Are those CDs expensive?
A I enjoy listening to music.
B I'm at the music shop.
C No, they're cheap.

5 Who's in the supermarket?
A They're doing a special offer.
B A lot of customers.
C There are so many clothes.

6 Let's sit on the bench.
A Yes, I'm getting a bit tired.
B Yes, it's very expensive.
C The escalator is just there.

4 **Rewrite the words to complete the gaps in the text.**

I'm looking at a picture of a bookshop. The shop is very (1) ___________ (**sbyu**) and there are a lot of (2) ___________ (**ersmustco**) shopping. There are a boy and a girl in the shop. The girl is (3) ___________ (**neingyoj**) looking at books. The boy isn't feeling happy – he is (4) ___________ (**ttgineg**) tired. I think he wants to take the (5) ___________ (**rotaaclse**) or the (6) ___________ (**ftli**) and go home! There are so many books in the shop! I don't think the books are (7) ___________(**nepevisex**). They are having a sale at the moment, so they are (8) ___________ (**aechp**).

Grammar 1

G

Present continuous

Look again at *Grammar database 5* on page 147 before doing these exercises.

1 Put a line through the incorrect sentence.

1 They are having lunch now. / They are have lunch now.
2 I'm not feel tired. / I'm not feeling tired.
3 Are they enjoying their dinner? / They are enjoying their dinner?
4 'Is he having fun?' 'No, he isn't.' / 'No, he doesn't.'
5 Is he look for clothes? / Is he looking for clothes?
6 She picking a flower. / She's picking a flower.
7 We are not shopping at the moment. / We not shopping at the moment.
8 'Are you eating?' 'Yes, I do.' / 'Yes, I am.'

2 Put the words into the correct order to make sentences or questions.

1 you / Are / bored? / feeling ______________________
2 a / are / We / playing / game. / computer ______________________
3 not / dinner. / eating / It's / its ______________________
4 I / eggs. / am / collecting ______________________
5 now. / homework / their / are / doing / They / not ______________________
6 grocer's? / shopping / Is / the / at / he ______________________

3 Rewrite to make questions and negative sentences.

1 I'm having lunch at the moment.
Am I having lunch at the moment? *I'm not having lunch at the moment.*

2 You're watching TV now.
______________________ ______________________

3 He's out shopping right now.
______________________ ______________________

4 They're feeling unhappy.
______________________ ______________________

5 We're having a sale right now.
______________________ ______________________

6 Marta is looking for new shoes.
______________________ ______________________

4 Answer the questions from Exercise 3 using short answers.

1 No, ____________.
2 Yes, ____________.
3 Yes, ____________.
4 No, ____________.
5 No, ____________.
6 Yes, ____________.

Wordpower!

1 Choose the correct word or phrase.

1 My little brother's socks are very small – they're **tiny / gigantic**!
2 His watch is round – it's **circular / narrow**.
3 The book I'm looking at is black and **triangular / thin**.
4 The shopping centre in my town is big – it's **little / huge**!
5 Her new TV is **triangular / square** and **flat / thick**.
6 A lift is usually big and **little / rectangular**.
7 Her skirt is a bit **circular / large**.
8 That music shop is **gigantic / round** – look at all the CDs!

Listening

CD Track 3

1 Listen to a conversation between a customer and an assistant and decide if these statements are true (T) or false (F).

1 The girl is shopping in the morning. T/F
2 The girl is in a florist's shop. T/F
3 The girl doesn't want to spend a lot of money. T/F
4 The shop is doing a special offer. T/F
5 The skirt is ten pounds. T/F
6 The girl buys the jeans. T/F

CD Track 3

2 Listen to the conversation again and complete the gaps.

1 The girl is shopping for her ____________'s party.
2 The party is next ____________.
3 The girl's favourite colour is ____________.
4 The skirt matches the girl's new ____________.
5 The jeans are ____________ pounds.
6 The girl gives the assistant ____________ pounds.

Grammar 2 G

Pronouns

Look again at *Grammar database 6* on page 147 before doing these exercises.

1 Write the reflexive pronoun that matches each pronoun.

1 me ____________
2 you ____________
3 you (plural) ____________
4 him ____________
5 her ____________
6 it ____________
7 us ____________
8 them ____________

2 Write a word in each gap to complete the sentences.

1 **A:** Amy, do you like ____________ **(these / this)** skirt?
B: No, but I like ____________ **(that / those)** one over there.

2 **A:** I need some of ____________ **(these / this)** carrots, please.
B: Do you want any of ____________ **(that / those)** tomatoes over there?

3 **A:** Are you doing a special offer on ____________ **(these / that)** jeans at the moment?
B: No, but ____________ **(those / this)** red skirts are half-price.

4 **A:** Excuse me. Is ____________ **(that / this)** your bike over there?
B: No, ____________ **(this / that)** is my bike right here.

3 Read the text and for each question, choose the correct answer, A, B or C.

I love shopping. I'm always looking for special offers on things like jeans, skirts and shoes. I love buying things for (1) ___ but my favourite thing to do is buy things for my friends and my family. My parents never buy things for (2) ___, so it's great fun buying them presents. I usually shop when they are having a sale at the shopping centre. That's why I'm here today! (3) ___ is a great shopping centre – it's huge! See (4) ___ shoe shop over there? All their shoes are half-price! And (5) ___ two bookshops there have always got cheap books. Wait! Let's go in here. (6) ___ is a great toy shop. Oh, look at (7) ___ little toy animals. Aren't (8) ___ lovely? Look! This little kitten is washing (9) ___! I may buy (10) ___ for my brother.

	A	B	C
1	**A** me	**B** myself	**C** I
2	**A** themselves	**B** ourselves	**C** herself
3	**A** These	**B** Those	**C** This
4	**A** this	**B** these	**C** that
5	**A** those	**B** that	**C** this
6	**A** Itself	**B** It	**C** These
7	**A** these	**B** this	**C** that
8	**A** they	**B** themselves	**C** them
9	**A** yourselves	**B** itself	**C** myself
10	**A** it	**B** that	**C** these

Quick check

4 Choose the correct answer.

1 We use the present continuous to talk about things happening now. **yes / no**
2 We often use *now*, *right now* and *at the moment* with the present continuous. **yes / no**
3 Which one is correct? **They're not having lunch. / They aren't having lunch. / both**
4 Which one is correct? **He's shopping now. / He is shop now. / both**
5 We use a **noun / pronoun / both** in place of nouns to sound more natural.
6 Which one is correct? Let's buy **us / ourselves** new T-shirts.
7 Do we use the demonstrative pronouns *that* and *those* when the object is near to us? **yes / no**
8 Which one is correct? **I need those book over there. / I need that book over there. / both**

Writing

1 Look at the picture and answer the questions.

1 What is the boy looking at?

____

2 What is the girl looking at?

____

3 Are the boy and girl enjoying themselves?

____

4 Is the shop assistant enjoying himself?

____

2 Complete the text with the verbs in the correct form.

This is a picture of a clothes shop – it looks like an expensive shop and I don't think they (1) ____________ (**have**) a sale. I think this clothes shop is in a large shopping centre in a town or in a city. The shop is very busy and a lot of people (2) ____________ (**go**) in and out of the shop. A boy and a girl are in the shop. I think they are twelve or thirteen years old. They (3) ____________ (**look**) at some clothes. The girl (4) ____________ (**wear**) a T-shirt and jeans. She (5) ____________ (**look**) at some skirts and the boy is looking at some socks. I think the girl (6) ____________ (**buy**) things for herself. I don't think the boy is buying things for himself. I think he (7) ____________ (**get**) some good ideas for presents for friends and family. The boy and girl look like they (8) ____________ (**enjoy**) themselves. Next to the lift in the picture, there is a shop assistant. I think he (9) ____________ (**feel**) tired or bored. He (10) ____________ (**not have**) fun. I don't think he likes his job, or the customers!

4

Read All About It!

Reading

1 Read the website and for each question, choose the correct answer, A, B or C.

www.highlandmiddleschool.org/pupil_website/calendar

Home | School news | Calendar | Short stories | Articles and reviews | Letters to the Editor

Highland Middle School
Pupil Website

Welcome to our calendar section!

This week we've got an exciting list of events for you. It's the first week of spring and a busy week at the school! We're having our Spring Party this weekend. I'm sure everyone's coming to that! And our other big event is the school play! Students from Mrs Billing's class are the actors in this funny play. And they sing too, so don't miss it!

And don't forget – our school reporter, Stephen Mills, is doing an interview with our favourite (and only!) English teacher, Mr Manning. Stephen asks our great teacher some very interesting questions, such as why he's an English teacher and how he stays so happy teaching us! Sounds exciting!

Also, check out our film reviews and short stories sections this week for reviews of this week's new films and a new short story!

Calendar of Events:

Tuesday, 23 March
Wendy Castings gives her reviews of new films 'One Happy Day' and 'No More Money'.

Wednesday, 24 March
Roger Norton with another great story, 'The Scary House on Black Street'.

Thursday, 25 March
Interview with Mr Manning.

Friday, 26 March
Our school play 'Sing it loud!' Play starts at 7.30pm in the Grand Theatre on Taylor St.

Weekend of 27–28 March:

Saturday, 27 March
The Spring Party!, 2–7pm at Hyde Park. We welcome both students and parents!

Sunday, 28 March
The Highland Ponies play against the Baneberry Donkeys at Highland Field. Match begins at 2pm.

1 The website has got a section for students' mail.
A Right **B** Wrong **C** Doesn't say

2 The section that you can see here is the News section.
A Right **B** Wrong **C** Doesn't say

3 The first paragraph says it's the first week of school.
A Right **B** Wrong **C** Doesn't say

4 Highland Middle School has got one English teacher.
A Right **B** Wrong **C** Doesn't say

5 Stephen Mills is answering questions from Mr Manning.
A Right **B** Wrong **C** Doesn't say

6 Roger Norton is a student in Mrs Billing's class.
A Right **B** Wrong **C** Doesn't say

7 The Spring Party is happening at Highland Middle School.
A Right **B** Wrong **C** Doesn't say

8 The Highland Ponies play football every Sunday.
A Right **B** Wrong **C** Doesn't say

Wordpower!

2 Each of the words in bold is in the wrong sentence. Write a word in bold from another sentence to replace the incorrect one.

1 James is an **opinion** and he runs a newspaper. ________
2 My friend Mary is a **calendar** and she writes news stories. ________
3 The **review** says there are three big events this week. ________
4 Helen is doing an **editor** and she's going to ask some really good questions. ________
5 Her **interview** is that newspapers are a bit boring. ________
6 The **reporter** of the film says the film is very exciting and has got good actors. ________

3 Match to make sentences.

1 John is a reporter ___
2 I'm watching a programme ___
3 I'm reading a review ___
4 Jason is an editor ___
5 I'm looking at my calendar ___
6 My view on school websites is ___

a to see what I'm doing tomorrow.
b and he writes articles for a sports website.
c about last night's play.
d on TV about school websites.
e they are interesting to read.
f and he runs a newspaper in town.

4 Read the dialogue and for each question, choose the correct answer, A, B or C.

Frank: I'm here with Rick Jones, (1) ___ of our town newspaper, *The Daily*. Thank you for giving me this (2) ___ .

Rick Jones: You're welcome, Frank.

Frank: Rick, you've got a new section called 'School News'. Can you tell me about it?

Rick Jones: Sure. It's got information about school events. It's got a (3) ___ that tells students when events are happening. It's also got (4) ___ of plays and films in town. Our (5) ___ , Louis Stark, also writes stories for the new section. There's also a section for student (6) ___ about school activities – what they like, what they don't like.

Frank: It sounds very interesting! Well, good luck with the new section!

	A	B	C
1	**A** programme	**B** editor	**C** interview
2	**A** interview	**B** calendar	**C** review
3	**A** review	**B** programme	**C** calendar
4	**A** interviews	**B** reviews	**C** reporters
5	**A** reporter	**B** view	**C** editor
6	**A** calendars	**B** opinions	**C** interviews

Grammar 1

Question words

Look again at *Grammar database 7* on page 148 before doing these exercises.

1 Choose the correct word or phrase.

1 **Where / When** are you leaving for school?
2 **Which / Who** section do you prefer – reviews or opinions?
3 **How / How many** books have you got at home?
4 **Who / What** is your favourite writer?
5 **What time / Why** do you get up at six o'clock?
6 **How old / What** does Tom do at the newspaper?

2 Tick (✔) the correct sentences. Underline the mistake in the incorrect sentences and write the correct word.

1 How many is your little sister? ___ ____________
2 Where TV programmes do you like? ___ ____________
3 What old is your interview tomorrow? ___ ____________
4 Why do you read film reviews? ___ ____________
5 Who does Mrs Scott live? ___ ____________
6 How do you write an email? ___ ____________

3 Write questions using *who, what, where, when, how old,* and *how many,* as in the example.

1 My favourite actor is Daniel Radcliffe. *Who's your favourite actor?*
2 I go to school at eight o'clock. ____________
3 I'm thirteen years old. ____________
4 I've got two sisters. ____________
5 I live on Sloan Street. ____________
6 I read books and the school newspaper. ____________

4 Write a word from the box in each gap.

how • what • where • which • who • why

Carol: Hi, Anthony, I'm writing an article on what kids our age like to do in their free time. Can I ask you some questions?

Anthony: Sure.

Carol: Great! First, (1) ____________ old are you?

Anthony: I'm fourteen. I'll be fifteen in May.

Carol: OK, good to know. And (2) ____________ do you live?

Anthony: I live here in Camden. It's an area of London.

Carol: And tell me, (3) ____________ do you like to do in your free time?

Anthony: Oh, I like to read, play sports and watch TV.

Carol: Can you tell me (4) ____________ programmes on TV are your favourite ones?

Anthony: Well, I love *The X Factor* and *Britain's Got Talent*.

Carol: Oh, really? And (5) ____________ do you like those programmes?

Anthony: Because they're really fun to watch.

Carol: Great. OK, one last question … (6) ____________ is your favourite actor on TV?

Anthony: I guess that would be Ricky Gervais from *The Office*.

Carol: Oh, yeah, he's really funny! Well, Anthony, thanks for your time!

Anthony: You're welcome.

Wordpower!

1 **Write one letter in each gap to complete the words or phrases. The first letter is given to help you.**

1 If you know a language, you can do this with it. **s** ___ ___ ___ ___
2 If you say something that's not true, you do this. **l** ___ ___
3 If you say something very quietly, you do this. **w** ___ ___ ___ ___ ___ ___
4 When you have a conversation with someone, you do this with them. **t** ___ ___ ___
5 You do this when you say something loudly. **s** ___ ___ ___ ___
6 If you are scared, sometimes you do this. **s** ___ ___ ___ ___ ___
7 If you know how to use a clock, you can do this. **t** ___ ___ ___ the **t** ___ ___ ___

2 **Read the dialogues and choose the correct answer.**

Margie: Do you (1) **talk / speak** Spanish, Jay?
Jay: Why? Do you want me to (2) **say / tell** something in Spanish?
Margie: Well, can you (3) **speak / talk** about the weather?
Jay: No, I don't know the words.
Margie: Come on, don't (4) **say / lie**. I know you know some Spanish words.
Jay: No, I don't! I'm (5) **saying / telling** you the truth!
Margie: OK, OK! Don't (6) **shout / tell**. I believe you.

Ellen: My little sister always (7) **whispers / screams** when she's excited. She's so loud!
Peter: Ha, ha! My little brother is different. He sometimes (8) **shouts / whispers** things so you can't hear him.
Ellen: I like that! I'd like to see them (9) **say / talk** to each other!

Listening

CD Track 4

1 **Listen to the beginning of this conversation and choose the correct word or phrase.**

1 The review is about a **school play / concert**.
2 The review is **on a website / in a newspaper**.
3 **Brenda / Thomas** is the writer of the review.

CD Track 5

2 **Listen to the complete conversation and for each question, choose the correct answer, A, B or C.**

1 Brenda thinks the film *Talk of the Town* is …
A very good. **B** not good. **C** very funny.
2 Brenda thinks the review of *Talk of the Town* is …
A very good. **B** wrong. **C** not good.
3 Thomas says the good thing about *White Nights* is …
A how long it is. **B** the kind of story. **C** the actors.
4 Thomas likes sad films that …
A have good stories. **B** are really long. **C** a bit boring.
5 Brenda prefers to watch films that are …
A sad. **B** happy. **C** different.

Grammar 2

G

too* and *very

Look again at *Grammar database 8* on page 148 before doing these exercises.

1 Tick (✔) the correct sentences. Underline the mistake in the incorrect sentences and write the correct word.

1 This question's too difficult – but I know the answer. ___ __________
2 You're talking too fast – I can't understand you. ___ __________
3 This book's very long – I can't finish it. ___ __________
4 This article's too short, but it doesn't need more words. ___ __________
5 This jacket's very small, but I can wear it. ___ __________
6 I'm too tired, but I'm going out to play. ___ __________

2 Write sentences using *too*, as in the example.

1 Chinese is very hard and I can't learn it. *Chinese is too hard to learn.*
2 Mrs Niles is very old and she can't ski. __________
3 The article's very short and we can't use it. __________
4 She's very young and she can't have a car. __________
5 Evan writes very badly and they can't read his work. __________
6 It's very early and we can't go to bed. __________

3 Read the dialogue and choose the correct word or phrase.

Diane: What do you think of Martin's maths article on the new school website, Paul?

Paul: Hmm. Well, it's over 2,000 words long. It's (1) **very / too** long to read!

Diane: Yes, I know. But he writes very (2) **good / well**, don't you think?

Paul: I'm sure he does. He's (3) **too / very** smart and I like Martin a lot. But maths is too difficult (4) **for me to / that I** do.

Diane: Yeah, OK. Do you like the poems on the website?

Paul: Yes, I do. The poems are very (5) **good / well** and I love reading them. And they're (6) **too / very** short, so you can read them very (7) **quick / quickly**.

Diane: Do you know who's writing these poems?

Paul: No, I don't. Do you?

Diane: Yes … it's me!

Paul: Why don't you write your name?

Diane: I'm (8) **too / very** scared to write it! If people think the poems are bad, I don't want them to know I'm writing them!

Quick check

4 Choose the correct answer.

1 Do we use question words to ask questions where the answer is yes or no? **yes / no**
2 Which is correct? **When do you live? / Where do you live? / both**
3 Which is correct? **Who's your maths teacher? / What's your maths teacher? / both**
4 Can we use *very* for negative things? **yes / no**
5 Can we use *too* to describe something positive or negative? **yes / no**
6 Which is correct? **This article's too long but I like it. / This article's very long but I like it. / both**

Writing

1 Match the questions with the correct answers to make an interview with a famous actor.

Interview with Kenneth Green
The famous actor Kenneth Green answers our questions.

1	Who is your favourite actor?	
2	How old are you?	
3	Where do you live?	
4	Why do you live there?	
5	When do you usually start work in the morning?	
6	How do you choose a good film?	
7	Of your two best films, which film do you prefer – *The Face* or *The Last Teacher*?	
8	When can we see your next film?	

a At six o'clock. I wake up very early!
b This summer. I'm in *Sports Story*, a film about a football player.
c *The Last Teacher*. It's a fun film!
d 27.
e Because it's lovely and it's in the centre of London.
f Well, there are many actors I like. I think Ian McKellen is my favourite. He's a very good actor!
g In London. My house is in the area of Covent Garden.
h I think about the story in the film. If I love it, then it's a film I want to be in.

2 Look at the questions and answers. Rewrite the answers using short answers. Use the short answers from exercise 1 as examples to follow.

1 Where do you live? I live in Covent Garden. *In Covent Garden.*
2 How old are you? I'm fifteen years old. ______
3 Why do you live in London? I live there because it's lovely. ______
4 When do you usually wake up? I wake up at eight o'clock. ______
5 When can we see your next film? My next film comes out this spring. ______
6 Which film do you prefer – *The Game* or *Summer Love*?
I prefer *The Game*. ______

Check your progress! | Units 3-4

1 **Read the text and for each question, choose the correct answer, A, B or C.**

Greg: Joanne, what are you doing?

Joanne: I'm reading a (1) ___ of a play at the Grand Theatre.

Greg: Oh, yes. I've seen it. In my (2) ___, it was a very good play.

Joanne: Well, I'm glad to hear that. I'm (3) ___ tired of bad plays!

Greg: Listen, do you want to go with me to the shopping centre later today?

Joanne: Oh, I don't know. I don't really like going to the shopping centre. There are so many (4) ___ walking around there, and the shops are so (5) ___. It's very loud too. Everyone's always (6) ___!

Greg: It's not that bad. They've got lots of (7) ___ things and I haven't got much money.

Joanne: Let's go to the bookshop then. I want to buy a nice (8) ___ book for my holidays.

Greg: Oh, where are you going?

Joanne: My family and I are going to Spain next week.

Greg: Oh, great! Well, I hope you (9) ___ yourself!

Joanne: Thanks! Now let's go shopping and get a good book!

1 **A** reporter **B** calendar **C** review
2 **A** programme **B** opinion **C** interview
3 **A** speaking **B** enjoying **C** getting
4 **A** customers **B** lifts **C** escalators
5 **A** flat **B** thin **C** busy
6 **A** lying **B** whispering **C** shouting
7 **A** huge **B** cheap **C** wide
8 **A** thick **B** square **C** round
9 **A** speak **B** say **C** enjoy

9 marks

2 **Put the verbs into the present continuous.**

'Hi, George, it's Paul. Martin and I (10) ___________ (**go**) to the music shop. Do you want to come? We (11) ___________ (**walk**) down Walter Street at the moment. Martin (12) ___________ (**eat**) a really good sandwich from the baker's. I (13) ___________ (**wear**) my T-shirt from Spain. We (14) ___________ (**have**) a very nice time. We (15) ___________ (**turn**) onto Main Street right now. Oh, there's John! He (16) ___________ (**stand**) by the bus stop. Now he (17) ___________ (**wave**) at us. Call me when you get this message. Bye!'

8 marks

3 **Choose the correct word or phrase.**

18 Janet is buying **herself / hers** a new TV.
19 It's Ben and Rachel's birthday. Let's get **them / themselves** something.
20 I like these shirts. How much are **them / they**?
21 That's not your pencil. It's **mine / my**.
22 **How many / What time** people are coming to the party?
23 **Why / What** does your dad drive you to school?
24 **When / How** do you do your homework so fast?
25 This book's **too / very** boring but I have to read it for school.

8 marks

Total:____ **/ 25 marks**

5

The Travel Bug!

Reading

1 Read the text about Zara's trip and for each question, choose the correct answer, A, B or C.

1 Zara is writing …
  A a blog.
  B in a diary.
  C a poem.

2 Zara was away …
  A on July 22nd.
  B a week ago.
  C for two weeks.

3 Zara writes about …
  A some of the trip.
  B most of the trip.
  C all of the trip.

4 Zara can't believe …
  A Buffalo was nice.
  B she went to Buffalo.
  C she's home.

2 Read the text again and decide if the statements are true (T) or false (F).

1 Zara was on holiday for seven days. T/F
2 Zara is from England. T/F
3 Zara went to Buffalo with four other people. T/F
4 Zara got to Buffalo early in the morning. T/F
5 Buffalo's roads have got a lot of cars on them. T/F
6 Buffalo isn't very big. T/F
7 Zara's hotel wasn't cheap. T/F
8 Zara was on the ferry for an hour. T/F
9 Siobhan was unhappy on the tour. T/F
10 Zara got her friend a present. T/F

Saturday, July 22nd

Hello! I was very busy last week, so I didn't have a minute to write until today. Don't be unhappy – I'm here now! I want to tell you about my trip to Buffalo, USA. I can't believe I was there – and for a whole week. Buffalo was amazing! The people were very nice and, of course, they speak English like we do here in London, England. Here's what I did on my holiday.

Mum, Dad, my cousin Siobhan and I arrived on Friday night at eleven o'clock – I was very tired, but very excited. We got a taxi to the Holiday Hotel. It's in the centre of the city, so it was easy to find. There was a lot of traffic, though. Buffalo isn't the capital city of the USA, but it is a huge city. Our hotel was nice and very close to the sights we wanted to visit. It was expensive – Dad wasn't very happy about that!

The next day, on Saturday, we went on a tour of the Niagara River. It was a forty-five minute tour and it was fantastic. Siobhan doesn't like ferries, so she didn't have fun at all! She likes shopping, though, so after the tour we went to a gigantic shopping centre. I got a very nice T-shirt – it's got a picture of Buffalo on it. I also got some postcards for my best friend, Safi. We went to explore the city and saw lots of really tall buildings. There were tourists everywhere but it was a great day.
I'm feeling tired now – more tomorrow!

Wordpower!

3 Write a word from the box in each gap.

capital • guide • sights • tickets • tour • tourists • traffic • trip • view

1 I went to New York – there were noisy ____________ everywhere!
2 The hotel is very close to the many ____________ I want to visit.
3 There's a lot of ____________ today. The roads are very busy.
4 What is the ____________ city of the UK?
5 How many ____________ have you got for the play?
6 We were right at the top, so the ____________ of the river was fantastic!
7 We didn't have a tour ____________ to tell us about the old buildings.
8 Did you have fun on your ____________ to Washington?
9 Welcome! I hope you enjoy today's ____________ of Greenwich Village.

4 Each of the words in bold is in the wrong sentence. Write a word in bold from another sentence to replace the incorrect one.

1 There are so many **guide** to visit in New York! ____________
2 There's always a lot of **tour** on this road in the morning. ____________
3 The **trip** arrived late at night – they were very tired. ____________
4 Our tour **tickets** is telling us about the city. ____________
5 When did you go on your **tourists** to America? ____________
6 We need to get three **sights** for the concert. ____________
7 Petros, what's the **view** city of the USA? ____________
8 I'm right at the top of the building, so I've got an amazing **capital** of the lake. ____________
9 Let's go on a **traffic** of Washington. ____________

Grammar 1

Past simple: basic irregular verbs

Look again at *Grammar database 9* on page 148 before doing these exercises.

1 Write the past simple of these verbs.

1 be ____________
2 come ____________
3 give ____________
4 get ____________
5 go ____________
6 have ____________
7 make ____________
8 see ____________
9 take ____________
10 do ____________

2 Match each question (1–10) with an answer (a–j).

1 Where was she last night? ___
2 When did you come to New York? ___
3 What did you give her for her birthday? ___
4 What time did they get to their hotel? ___
5 Where did your cousin, Bob, go last week? ___
6 When did we have dinner? ___
7 What did she make for lunch? ___
8 What did you see at the top of the Empire State Building? ___
9 Did you take any photographs? ___
10 When did you do your homework? ___

a She was at a concert.
b We saw the river and lots of ferries.
c Yes, I took thousands!
d I came three days ago.
e He went to Washington.
f They got there at about half past eleven.
g She made hot dogs!
h I gave her a ticket for a play.
i I did it an hour ago.
j We had dinner an hour ago.

3 Write the verbs in the correct form.

Last week, my grandmother (1) __________ (**come**) to visit us in America. I'm very close to her, so it was lovely. And she (2) __________ (**give**) me a present – she always (3) __________ (**give**) me presents. She hasn't got a lot of money, but she loves shopping and getting people things. This present (4) __________ (**be**) very big, so I was very excited! It was a computer! Grandma (5) __________ (**get**) me my first computer! I was very happy when I (6) __________ (**see**) it and I immediately (7) __________ (**take**) it to my bedroom. Yesterday, I (8) __________ (**go**) to the florist's. They (9) __________ (**have**) some lovely flowers there and I got my grandmother twelve red ones. They (10) __________ (**make**) her feel very special.

4 Choose the correct word or phrase.

1 The tourists went on a tour **now / this morning**.
2 Did the tour guide come to your hotel **yesterday / at the moment**?
3 Mum made lunch **this afternoon / now**.
4 Did he take a lot of photos **right now / last week**?
5 I gave him his ferry ticket **this morning / at the moment**.
6 We had hot dogs for dinner **now / last night**.

Wordpower!

1 Complete the table with words from the box.

Austria • Brazil • China • Denmark • Egypt • France • Georgia
Hungary • India • Japan • Kenya • Latvia • Mexico • Norway
Oman • Poland • Qatar • Russia • Spain • Turkey • Ukraine
Venezuela • Wales • Yemen • Zimbabwe

Africa	Asia	Europe		North America
				South America

Listening

CD Track 6

1 Listen to three people talking about travel and for each question, choose the correct answer, A, B or C.

1 Tarak took a trip with all of his family.
A Right **B** Wrong **C** Doesn't say

2 Tarak's mum wants to go to Turkey again.
A Right **B** Wrong **C** Doesn't say

3 Claudia didn't have fun all the time on the bus tour.
A Right **B** Wrong **C** Doesn't say

4 The tour guide on Sylvie's bus made her sad.
A Right **B** Wrong **C** Doesn't say

5 Tom had lunch at the hotel every day.
A Right **B** Wrong **C** Doesn't say

6 Tom and Fritz went swimming a lot.
A Right **B** Wrong **C** Doesn't say

CD Track 6

2 Listen to the last speaker again and complete the gaps.

Name of hotel: *The Great (1) ____________*

Cost: *(2) € ____________ every night*

Place: *Centre of the (3) ____________*

24 Durban (4) ____________

Close to all the (5) ____________

Grammar 2

G

Past simple: regular verbs and more irregular verbs

Look again at *Grammar database 10* on page 149 before doing these exercises.

1 Match.

1 begin ___	**a** drove
2 drive ___	**b** said
3 eat ___	**c** found
4 find ___	**d** left
5 fly ___	**e** told
6 leave ___	**f** began
7 meet ___	**g** wrote
8 say ___	**h** met
9 tell ___	**i** visited
10 write ___	**j** flew
11 visit ___	**k** ate

2 Choose the correct word or phrase.

1 Bob and Marge **are visiting / visited** Poland last summer.

2 Did they enjoy their trip? Yes, they **did / did enjoy**.

3 Anetta **told / tell** her best friend about my hotel.

4 Did the tour **began / begin** an hour ago?

5 We **didn't visit / didn't visited** Washington on our tour.

6 I **didn't ate / didn't eat** my lunch.

7 He **writed / wrote** me a letter last night.

8 **Did he visited / Did he visit** you on Sunday?

3 Write the verbs in the past simple.

1 They ____________ (**drive**) all round the city yesterday.

2 Look! I ____________ (**find**) my camera.

3 Martha ____________ (**leave**) London yesterday. She's in New York now.

4 Kevin ____________ (**eat**) his hot dog an hour ago.

5 We ____________ (**fly**) back on a plane from Oman last night.

6 The tour guide ____________ (**tell**) the tourists a funny story.

7 I ____________ (**meet**) a nice girl on the ferry in Turkey.

8 The tour ____________ (**begin**) early in the morning.

4 **Read the text and for each question, choose the correct answer, A, B or C.**

	A	B	C
1	didn't you tell	didn't tell you	didn't told you
2	began	begin	begins
3	fly	flied	flew
4	find	finds	found
5	met	meet	meeted
6	tells	told	tell
7	drived	drove	drives
8	visited	visit	visits
9	didn't eat	didn't ate	not ate
10	I did say	Say I	Did I say

write reply send

Dear Miguel,
I can't believe I'm in India! I was very busy last week, so I (1) ___ about my trip. I want to tell you about it now, though! It (2) ___ two days ago. I (3) ___ on a huge plane from London to Mumbai. I was on the plane for a lot of hours. I (4) ___ a taxi and went to my hotel. I was very tired, so I immediately went to sleep. The next day I got up and went to the swimming pool. I (5) ___ a nice girl from America there. She (6) ___ me about some amazing sights in Mumbai and she had a car, so we (7) ___ all round the city and (8) ___ some of them – fantastic! Well, that's all for now. I (9) ___ lunch this afternoon, so I'm hungry. (10) ___ they've got delicious meals at my hotel?
Write soon,
Margarite

Quick check

5 **Choose the correct word or phrase.**

1 We use the past simple to talk about single complete events in the past. **yes / no**
2 We use both regular and irregular verbs in the past simple. **yes / no**
3 Which one is correct? **They were there yesterday. / They be there yesterday. / both**
4 Which one is correct? **Did Mum made this? / Did Mum make this?**
5 The past simple of *come* is **comed / came**.
6 Which one is correct? **Did you begin your trip yesterday? / Did you began your trip yesterday? / both**
7 We don't use **now / last week** with past simple.
8 Which one is correct? *Did you visit America?* **Yes, I was. / No, I didn't. / both**

Writing

1 **Read the text and for each question, choose the correct answer, A, B or C.**

1 What kind of text is it?
A a review of a play
B a postcard describing a place
C a scary short story
2 Who wrote the text?
A Giselle
B Giselle's dad
C Dominic
3 Where is Giselle?
A in a car
B in New York
C in California

2 **Read the text again and underline all the adjectives.**

Hello, Dominic!
California is fantastic! Last week, we drove from New York to California. We were in our tiny car for hours every day – it was so boring – and every night I was very tired. But now we're here and I am happy and very excited! America is a gigantic country and California is huge. It's very hot here now, but not too hot – I don't mind this weather, I think it's great. Our hotel is amazing. It has got a big, circular swimming pool – I go swimming a lot. I also eat a lot! The meals here at the hotel are delicious. My dad said they were expensive, but Mum told me they were cheap.
See you soon,
Giselle

Dominic Adams
121 Scotland Ave
Leeds
L20 4PT

6

Animal Magic!

Reading

http://www.worldofpets.co.uk

Home | Recent Posts | Archive | Links | About us

World of Pets!

Have you got a pet? Send us a blog entry and tell us your story! We'd love to hear all about it!

Maria, 12 Mexico City, Mexico
I've got two pet mice and their names are Luisa and Rosa. Luisa's white and she's got small red eyes and small feet. She's only about 2 months old. Rosa is a brown mouse. I'm not sure how old she is. All I know is that she's Luisa's mother! Luisa's father was a white mouse, so that's why she's white. I haven't got Luisa's father any more or her brothers and sisters because I gave them to my brother José. But I'm happy with just the mother and the daughter!

Joseph, 14 Melbourne, Australia
We've got three dogs in our family – Angel, Lulu and Coco. They're sisters actually! We got them when they were puppies, and they're three years old now. They like to run outside and play with the ball. They like to play inside the house too, but we don't usually let them inside. They usually stay out in the garden where they sleep and eat. When it's really cold in the winter, they can come inside and sleep in the living room. They're very good dogs, and I'm really glad we've got them.

Sue Li, 13 Hong Kong, China
I've got a strange pet – a butterfly! It's a very beautiful pet, with blue, green, black and white colours. I got a butterfly as a pet because my parents said no to dogs and cats. They don't like them because they say they're not good for the house. And we haven't got a big house or a big garden, so the only kind of pet I can have is a small one. I like butterflies because they are very interesting to look at. I got this one a few weeks ago, and I'm thinking of getting another one really soon.

1 Read the blog entries and for each question, choose the correct answer, A, B or C.

1 The blog entries are about animals …
A at zoos. **B** in homes. **C** in forests.

2 The website is for people from …
A Mexico. **B** Australia. **C** many places.

3 The website lets you ____ about animals.
A read **B** write **C** read and write

2 Read the entries again and write a word in each gap to complete the sentences.

1 The colour of Maria's pet mouse Rosa is ____________.
2 Maria gave Luisa's father to her ____________.
3 Joseph's family got their dogs when they were ____________.
4 Joseph's dogs sleep inside the house in the ____________.
5 Sue Li's parents said she can't have a cat or a ____________.
6 Sue Li thinks butterflies are very ____________ to watch.

Wordpower!

3 Match to make sentences.

1 When you lick something ___
2 Look at how cute ___
3 She's got a good memory ___
4 It's a fact ___
5 People's teeth grow ___
6 A crocodile loses over 3,000 teeth ___

a that elephants live for about 60 years.
b that mouse is!
c and she always remembers our names.
d in its lifetime.
e when they are children.
f you can taste it too.

4 For each question, choose the correct word, A, B or C.

1 My dog has got a great ___ for people.
A lifetime **B** fact **C** memory
2 Goldfish can remember things for months. That's an interesting …
A fact. **B** memory. **C** life.
3 People ___ a lot when they're young, but not when they're old.
A put **B** grow **C** taste
4 Mice can have lots and lots of baby mice in their …
A memory. **B** time. **C** lifetime.
5 My cat loves to ___ my hands.
A grow **B** eat **C** lick

5 Write a word from the box in each gap.

fact • grow • lick • lifetime • memory • sweet

Horses are amazing animals! They have a great (1) ___________ and they can remember people, places and things that happen to them during their whole (2) ___________. They are quite friendly too. They aren't often scared of people and they can (3) ___________ food from a person's hand while they stand in front of them. They are very (4) ___________ animals when they are young. They really like to play! They (5) ___________ quite fast and they become adults after about four or five years. An interesting (6) ___________ is that horses only sleep for about three hours a day, and they usually sleep while they are standing. Imagine people doing that! No need for beds!

Grammar 1

Regular and irregular plurals

Look again at *Grammar database 11* on page 149 before doing these exercises.

1 Tick (✔) the correct sentences. Underline the mistake in the incorrect sentences and write the correct word.

1 Both dogs and cats have got four leg. ___ ___________
2 The two child are playing with the ponies at the zoo. ___ ___________
3 How many fish are in this lake? ___ ___________
4 My uncle's got a lot of sheeps on his farm. ___ ___________
5 These box are for the animals to sleep in. ___ ___________
6 The horses sometimes eat all the cherry off the trees. ___ ___________

2 Write the words in bold in the correct form.

1 Who are the ___________ (**man**) that work at this zoo?
2 The mother lion is taking care of her two ___________ (**baby**).
3 How many ___________ (**kitten**) has your cat got?
4 When we become ___________ (**adult**), we stop growing.
5 Are those two ___________ (**woman**) part of the same family?
6 How many ___________ (**human**) are there in the world?

3 Write sentences in the plural.

1 Mouse / have got / four / foot ___________________________
2 Crocodile / have got / 70 / tooth ___________________________
3 Goldfish / have got / good / memory ___________________________
4 Puppy / have got / cute / face ___________________________
5 Fly / have got / small / mouth ___________________________
6 Many / animal / have got / tongue ___________________________

4 Write a word from the box in each gap in the plural.

butterfly • colour • country • day • garden • size

We often see (1) ___________ flying round in the spring. They fly round our (2) ___________ going from one flower to the next. They come in many beautiful (3) ___________, such as yellow, blue, red and orange, and a single butterfly has usually got three or four. They also come in different (4) ___________. Some are quite small, while others are large. It's the large ones that are often very beautiful. They sometimes travel through many different (5) ___________ in their lifetime. A butterfly that lives in Mexico in the winter flies to America and Canada when the weather becomes warm. So, when we see this butterfly in a northern country, we know the (6) ___________ are getting warmer and summer is on the way.

Wordpower!

1 Each of the words in bold is in the wrong sentence. Write a word in bold from another sentence to replace the incorrect one.

1 You can't **run** up an elephant – it's very big! ____________
2 You can **jump** this button and the animals will get food. ____________
3 Don't **pull** the puppy – keep it in your hands! ____________
4 That horse can **drop** really fast! ____________
5 If you see a crocodile in a river, just slowly **put** away! ____________
6 Mice are small but they can **walk** very high. ____________
7 This chick is very cute – I don't want to **pick** it down! ____________
8 Don't **push** our dog's tail – he gets very angry! ____________

2 Read the text and for each question, choose the correct answer, A, B or C.

Dogs and cats are wonderful pets, but they can be difficult sometimes. Dogs often (1) ___ around the house for hours and hours when they're excited. They can (2) ___ you down the street when you take them outside. Cats can (3) ___ all over your homework and get it dirty, and dogs can just eat it! Both dogs and cats can (4) ___ up on a table if there's food on it. And when you (5) ___ food on the floor and your dog's around, it's gone in seconds. A big dog can (6) ___ you down when it jumps on you! But really, we love both dogs and cats because they're fun to (7) ___ up and hold. And sometimes we never want to (8) ___ them down because we love them so much!

	A	B	C
1	**A** drop	**B** push	**C** run
2	**A** jump	**B** pull	**C** pick
3	**A** walk	**B** push	**C** drop
4	**A** push	**B** pick	**C** jump
5	**A** run	**B** drop	**C** push
6	**A** put	**B** push	**C** pick
7	**A** pick	**B** walk	**C** run
8	**A** jump	**B** push	**C** put

Listening

CD Track 7

1 Listen to the beginning of a conversation about pets and for each question, choose the correct answer, A or B.

1 Fran thinks pythons are …
A nice. **B** not nice.

2 Thomas thinks pythons are …
A cool. **B** scary.

3 Fran asks why Paul hasn't got a ___ for a pet.
A dog **B** cat

4 Thomas thinks ___ and cats are boring.
A goldfish **B** dogs

CD Track 8

2 Listen to the complete conversation and match each person with the pet they have. Three of the pets will not be used.

1 Paul ___
2 Fran ___
3 Thomas ___
4 Sasha ___
5 Ryan ___

a goldfish
b python
c dog
d cat
e monkey
f lizard
g butterfly
h mouse

Grammar 2

Articles

Look again at *Grammar database 12* on page 150 before doing these exercises.

1 Put the words into the correct order to make sentences.

1 gecko / pet. / is / A / interesting / an ____________________
2 is / animal. / aye-aye / a / strange / An ____________________
3 giraffe / the / an / There / adult / zoo. / at / is ____________________
4 park? / elephant / a / small / the / there / at / Is ____________________
5 enormous / There's / garden! / an / in / python / the ____________________
6 African / TV? / an / lion / on / Is ____________________

2 Read the dialogue and write *the* or – in the gaps. A dash (–) means no article is necessary.

Marcy: What are you doing at (1) __________ weekend, Paula?
Paula: I'm thinking about going to (2) __________ zoo on (3) __________ Sunday. They have (4) __________ elephants and they do a show. I love those animals! I really want to see (5) __________ elephants in that show.
Marcy: That sounds fun. I hear they've got (6) __________ African monkeys there too. I'd like to see (7) __________ monkeys there if you don't mind.
Paula: Of course. I like (8) __________ monkeys a lot too. They're (9) __________ funny animals. It should be fun!
Marcy: Good. So, shall we meet at (10) __________ ten o'clock?
Paula: Sounds great! I'm excited!

3 Read the text and for each question, choose the correct answer, A, B or C.

I really like the zoo in my city. I live in (1) ___ London and we've got (2) ___ amazing zoo. There are (3) ___ lions, elephants and monkeys that live in (4) ___ beautiful gardens. My favourite animals at the zoo are (5) ___ fish. They're very colourful and beautiful. I think (6) ___ fish are very interesting animals in general and I've got (7) ___ goldfish at my house – Ralph! I don't know if he's (8) ___ boy, but he's four years old, so I think he's probably (9) ___ adult now. Ralph's (10) ___ cool pet, but he's nothing like (11) ___ animals at the zoo. Oh well, I can always go to the zoo for (12) ___ hour or two when I like, so I'm happy about that!

1 **A** a **B** the **C** –
2 **A** a **B** an **C** the
3 **A** the **B** – **C** a
4 **A** – **B** a **C** an
5 **A** an **B** a **C** the
6 **A** the **B** a **C** –
7 **A** the **B** – **C** a
8 **A** – **B** a **C** an
9 **A** the **B** an **C** –
10 **A** a **B** the **C** –
11 **A** the **B** an **C** –
12 **A** a **B** the **C** an

Quick check

4 Choose the correct answer.

1 Do we use plurals when there is only one thing? **yes / no**
2 Do we use plurals when we think of things as a group? **yes / no / both**
3 Which is correct? **He's got a sheep. / He's got sheep. / both**
4 Do we use *a* and *an* with specific singular nouns? **yes / no**
5 Do we use *the* with plural nouns when we are talking generally? **yes / no**
6 Which is correct? **Today is 15th April. / Today is the 15th April. / both**

Writing

1 Read the note and for each question, choose the correct answer, A or B.

Hi, Gary,

Thank you so much for agreeing to look after Sam and Ricky this week. Here are some instructions so you know what to do:

- Give Sam his cat food once a day, in the morning. Put his food in the small red bowl in the kitchen.
- Give Ricky his dog food twice a day, once in the morning, once at night. Put his food in the black bowl in the garden.
- Take Ricky for a walk once a day. You can take him for a walk twice a day if you want.
- Don't forget to put water in both Sam's and Ricky's water bowls.
- Make sure their food is put away in the cupboard after you feed them.
- My bird Stiles has enough food and water, but you can say hi to him if you like. Just never let him out of his cage!

Don't forget to call if you have any trouble with anything! Thanks again, and see you next week!

Bye for now!

Love, Harriet

1	How long does Gary have to look after Harriet's pets?	**A** a weekend	**B** a week
2	What kind of pet is Sam?	**A** a cat	**B** a dog
3	How often does Ricky get his food?	**A** once a day	**B** twice a day
4	How many times a day does Gary have to walk the dog?	**A** once	**B** twice
5	What can Gary do with Stiles if he wants?	**A** let him out of the cage	**B** say hi to him

2 Write the imperative of each of these sentences.

1 You feed the dogs twice a day. ____________________
2 You play with the cat for twenty minutes. ____________________
3 You don't let the lizard out of his cage. ____________________
4 You make sure there's lots of water. ____________________
5 You don't forget to put the food away. ____________________

Check your progress! | Units 5-6

1 Write one word from the box in each gap.

Africa • facts • lick • lifetime • sights • trip • Zimbabwe

www.adeleblog.co.uk

Adele's Blog

Hi, everyone! Welcome to my blog. Wow! I can't believe I am in (1) __________! It's a huge continent and (2) __________ is a lovely country. I'm having a great time on my (3) __________ so far. Here's what I did during the first few days here. We arrived on Saturday, but it was too late to go and visit the (4) __________. On Sunday morning our tour guide arrived at the hotel and took us to see some strange animals. We saw some crocodiles! She told us some interesting (5) __________ about them. A crocodile's tongue is stuck to the bottom of its mouth, so it can eat you, but it can't (6) __________ you! Oh, and she told us that a crocodile's teeth fall out all the time. A crocodile grows about 3,000 teeth in its (7) __________!

7 marks

2 Choose the correct word or phrase.

8 The **childs / children** went to the park yesterday.
9 Let's go on a tour at **the / a** weekend.
10 Did he tell you his birthday is on **– / at** Monday?
11 Oh, no! There are two **mice / mouses** in my bedroom.
12 I spent **an / a** hour feeding the chicks and ducks.
13 We arrived in New York at **– / the** eight o'clock.
14 Did you eat **cherries / cherrys** for lunch?
15 That crocodile has got lots of **tooths / teeth**!

8 marks

3 Rewrite to make questions and negative sentences.

16 Mum and Dad flew to India last week.

__________ __________

17 You and Tom were late for the tour this morning.

__________ __________

18 You made hot dogs for dinner last night.

__________ __________

19 Hans and Peter went to visit Times Square at five o'clock.

__________ __________

20 Betty was in the capital city of the USA this summer.

__________ __________

10 marks

Total:____ / 25 marks

7

At the Airport!

Reading

1 Read the article and match the people to what they do (a–g). There is one letter you do not need to use.

They Work so Airports Work!

When I was a child, like many little boys and girls, I wanted to be a pilot. It was my dream to fly all round the world in a big expensive plane. Well, I'm an adult now, and I'm not a pilot – I'm a reporter – and today I'm writing about the different interesting jobs there are in airports.

First, let's talk a bit more about pilots. Of course, they fly the planes but they do a lot more than that. Pilots need to like other people and they need to enjoy helping them and talking to them.

Then, there are the flight attendants. Can you imagine being on a plane and there wasn't a flight attendant to help you? You can't, can you? A flight attendant is there to help you during the flight. A good flight attendant gets the passengers food or drinks and explains to them how to stay safe on the plane.

Pilots and flight attendants have what I like to call 'sky jobs'. But what about the people who have 'ground jobs'? Let's look at an airport mechanic's job. A mechanic works on all the different parts of the plane – the engine, the body, the wings – and tells the pilot that the plane is fine to leave the ground.

Security guards work on the ground too. They've got a very important job at the airport. They look at passengers' passports to make sure they are who they say they are. They also look very carefully at passengers' baggage – they use a scanner, so they can see what people have got in their bags.

Airports need all of these people, so passengers are safe when they fly from place to place. Pilots, flight attendants, mechanics and security guards work so airports work!

People

1 Pilot ___
2 Flight attendant ___, ___
3 Mechanic ___
4 Security guard ___, ___

What they do

a serves people on the plane
b checks the plane for problems
c flies the plane
d checks who people are
e cooks food for the people on the plane
f gives instructions to passengers
g looks at what people have with them

2 Read the article again and write a word or short phrase to answer each question.

1 What did the writer want to be when he was young? ___________
2 What job does the writer do now? ___________
3 When does a flight attendant help people? ___________
4 Who tells the pilot the plane is fine? ___________
5 What helps security guards know who people are? ___________
6 What does a security guard use to check baggage? ___________

Wordpower!

3 Write a word in each gap to complete the sentences. The first letter is given to help you.

1 I'm going to the airport early to make sure I **c**__________ my plane.
2 I always feel strange when the plane I'm on **t**__________ **o**__________.
3 Thousands of **p**__________ pass through this airport every week.
4 I'm a flight attendant. I tell people how to stay **s**__________ on the plane.
5 Look, I've got a new **p**__________. My photograph is lovely, isn't it?
6 The security guard is using that scanner to check our **b**__________.
7 Tell me what to do in an **e**__________.
8 Please sit down, sir. The plane is **l**__________.

4 For each question, choose the correct answer, A or B.

1 That ___ is talking to the pilot of the plane.
A baggage **B** passenger
2 It's quite late. I hope Bob ___ his plane.
A catches **B** takes off
3 I'm a pilot. Part of my job is to ___ the plane carefully.
A land **B** catch
4 My grandfather doesn't like planes. He thinks they aren't …
A emergency. **B** safe.
5 I always scream when the plane ___ – it scares me!
A takes off **B** catches
6 Give the security guard your ___, Boris.
A emergency **B** passport
7 Why do you need all that ___ for a weekend trip?
A passengers **B** baggage
8 Please come to my house – it's a(n) ___!
A emergency **B** passenger

Grammar 1

G

Countable and uncountable nouns

Look again at *Grammar database 13* on page 150 before doing these exercises.

1 Write C for countable noun and U for uncountable noun.

1 airport ___
2 people ___
3 plane ___
4 baggage ___
5 attendant ___
6 passport ___
7 water ___
8 information ___
9 furniture ___
10 pilot ___
11 music ___
12 mechanic ___
13 advice ___
14 air ___
15 drink ___
16 metre ___

2 Write a word or phrase from the box in each gap.

a coffee • a hair • coffee • hair • time • times • travel • travels

1 I want you to tell me about your __________ in India!
2 Flight attendant! There's __________ in my soup!
3 I don't have __________ to help you.
4 Mechanics have short __________ for safety reasons.
5 Let's go to that little place over there and get __________ .
6 She loves her job, but there are __________ when she feels a bit bored.
7 Oh no! There isn't any __________ for Bill to drink with his breakfast.
8 My wife and I enjoy __________ . We go to a different country every year.

3 Read the text and choose for each question, choose the correct answer, A, B or C.

You like airports, so you think you want (1) ___ working for a big airline. Let me give you some (2) ___ . Airports are exciting – they are like a small city with lots of (3) ___ coming and going – but to work at an airport you need to enjoy helping (4) ___ and the other men and (5) ___ that work at the airport. You also need to know what you want to do at the airport. Do you want to be (6) ___ and fly a plane? Do you want to be a mechanic and check for problems with the plane's engine, wings and (7) ___ ? Or do you want to be a flight attendant and serve food, (8) ___ and other (9) ___ on the plane?

Call 218-5555 for (10) ___ about working for us at Stanwick Airport. We might have a job that works for you!

	A	B	C
1	jobs	job	a job
2	advice	an advice	advices
3	peoples	a people	people
4	a passenger	passenger	passengers
5	women	a woman	woman
6	pilots	a pilot	pilot
7	a body	body	bodies
8	coffee	coffees	a coffee
9	a drink	drink	drinks
10	information	informations	an information

Wordpower!

1 Write a word in each gap to complete the sentences.

1 That box is made of ___________ and that T-shirt is made of ___________.
cotton **cardboard**

2 Planes are usually made of ___________ and houses are often made of ___________.
metal **wood**

3 My shoes are made of ___________ and my socks are made of ___________.
leather **cotton**

4 The child's little plane is made of ___________. It's safe to play with – it's not made of ___________.
glass **plastic**

5 This is my dad's watch. It's not made of ___________. It's made of ___________, leather and metal.
glass **rubber**

2 Choose the correct word to complete the text.

Hello and thank you for flying with us today. In *Airline Magazine* there are some interesting ideas for presents for those at home. Let me tell you about some of our special offers. First, for the children, we've got these cute little planes. The plane's wings are made of (1) **plastic / glass** and the plane's body is made of (2) **cotton / metal.** These planes are fun, and safe to play with.
Here I've got men's watches. Look! This part is made of (3) **glass / wood** and this part is made of real (4) **rubber / leather**. And here I've got women's socks – look at the amazing colours! They're made of (5) **wood / cotton**, so they aren't expensive – very nice! And, of course, there are these (6) **metal / cardboard** postcards for all your friends and family to enjoy.

Listening

CD Track 9

1 Listen to three people talking about planes and airports. Match the speakers with the statements. There is one letter you do not need to use.

1 Speaker 1 ___
2 Speaker 2 ___
3 Speaker 3 ___

a made a mistake and didn't catch a plane.
b doesn't want to be a passenger.
c had a problem with his/her baggage.
d was excited when the plane took off.

CD Track 9

2 Listen again and choose the correct word.

1 Sophia is from **Portugal / Egypt**.
2 Sophia spent time on the plane looking at **magazines / passengers**.
3 Vincenzo was in Greece for **two / five** weeks.
4 Vincenzo arrived at the airport on May **fifth / sixth**.
5 Fernando's **parents / grandmother** doesn't enjoy travelling.

Grammar 2

G

Quantitative adjectives (*some, any, many, much, a lot of, no*)

Look again at *Grammar database 14* on page 150 before doing these exercises.

1 For each question, choose the correct answer, A or B.

		A	B
1	Do you have ___ tickets for Flight 410?	**A** no	**B** any
2	That airline doesn't have ___ planes on the ground right now.	**A** many	**B** much
3	We've got ___ food, so you're welcome to stay for dinner.	**A** a lot of	**B** any
4	We have ___ coffee in the house for breakfast.	**A** any	**B** no
5	I haven't got ___ money, but we can fly to Buffalo.	**A** much	**B** any
6	A flight attendant hasn't got ___ time to sit and relax.	**A** no	**B** any

2 Complete the tables with words and phrases from the boxes. Be careful! You need to use some of the words and phrases twice.

any • no • some

positive statements	(1)
	(2)
negative statements	(3)
questions	(4)

a lot of • many • much

countable nouns	(5)
	(6)
uncountable nouns	(7)
	(8)

3 Complete the text with one word for each gap.

write reply send

Hello, Sacha!
I'm at an airport in New York City waiting for my flight to Warsaw. It is a very busy airport and there are a (1)__________ of people coming and going – it's like a small city! Yesterday, I took a plane from Buffalo to New York City. The plane was very small and (2) __________ of the passengers were scared when we took off. There was a flight attendant on the plane, but there wasn't (3)__________ food at all! I had some fruit in my bag, so I wasn't too unhappy. And there wasn't (4)__________ water – or I don't think there was. I wanted (5)__________ water and the flight attendant gave me this tiny little glass of it. Then I wanted some coffee, but she said there wasn't (6)__________. Isn't that strange? I don't think there are (7)__________ airlines that don't serve things to eat, or coffee. I wanted to call you last night, but I had (8)__________ money for the phone. You know, this is my first trip to Warsaw, so I wanted you to tell me about (9)__________ interesting sights Warsaw has got. Oh, and have you got (10)__________ advice for me about good hotels?
Write back soon,
Timmy

Quick check

4 Choose the correct answer.

1 Uncountable nouns often refer to ideas or materials. **yes / no**
2 *Advice* and *baggage* are uncountable nouns. **yes / no**
3 *Hair* and *coffee* are **countable nouns / uncountable nouns / both**.
4 Which one is correct? Your information **is / are** correct.
5 Which one is correct? I've got **some / any** money.
6 Which is correct? **I've got a lot of water. / I've got a lot of friends. / both**
7 We use a*ny* in **negative statements / questions / both**.
8 We use **much / many** with uncountable nouns.

Writing

1 Complete the description with phrases from the box.

on the right • in the background • in the foreground • on the left

This is a picture of a scene in an airport. It is a very busy airport and there are a lot of passengers coming and going.

(1) ___________, some people are sleeping – perhaps they are waiting for a flight. They have got a lot of baggage. It is all around them.

(2) ___________, there are a lot of passengers. They look tired. Perhaps their plane landed a short time ago. They are waiting for their baggage.

(3) ___________, there are people eating and drinking coffee and other drinks. Perhaps they are waiting for a flight, or they might be waiting for planes to land.

(4) ___________, there is a security guard. He is talking to a passenger. He is checking her passport to see that she is who she says she is. Perhaps she is at the airport to catch a plane.

2 For each question, choose the correct answer, A, B or C.

1 What is the best title for the description?
A A Long Trip
B An Airport Scene
C No Passengers

2 Paragraph 1 describes …
A what is in the back of the picture.
B something that is missing from the picture.
C the scene in general.

8

Lucky Escapes!

Reading

1 Read the newspaper articles and for each question, choose the correct answer, A, B or C.

a A strange accident happened at Mitchell's department store yesterday. A car drove into the front window and landed inside the shop. For some reason, the driver fell asleep while he was driving the car. The man woke up when the car went through the window. Shoppers were quite scared by the accident, but they ran before the car hit the window. The driver was very lucky that no-one was hurt in the accident.

1 The driver fell asleep …
A after the accident. **B** during the accident.
C before the accident.

b A bus had an accident this morning on the corner of Long Street and Queen Street. The bus driver was talking on his mobile phone when the accident happened. He drove the bus off Long Street and into a newspaper stand. Ten people were waiting for the bus at the time of the accident and there were five people who were sitting on the bus. No-one was hurt.

2 The bus driver was talking on his mobile phone …
A before the accident. **B** at the time of the accident.
C both before and at the time of the accident.

c Bad weather caused many accidents around town this morning. A car crash happened in the Forest Grove area at 8.35am. A woman was driving her car when another car hit her from behind. Another accident happened in the city centre at 9.15am when a truck drove into a car. The driver wasn't able to see where he was going. A third accident happened on High Street at 11.05am when the driver hit a tree that was lying in the street.

3 Which accident had only one car?
A the first **B** the second **C** the third

d Actor Julian Law nearly had an accident on his boat today. He was sailing in Greece when bad weather caused problems. At the time there were two other boats near him and the weather caused the boats to move closer. The two other boats hit each other, but Law's boat was all right. After 20 minutes, the weather got better and Law was able to make it back to land safely.

4 Law travelled back to land …
A when the weather got bad.
B when the two boats hit each other.
C when the weather got better.

e Actor Luke Grant was in an accident today while walking through Kensington Park. A man on a bicycle was trying to take a picture of him. When the man got close to Grant, he fell off his bike and onto Grant. Both fell to the ground. The accident didn't upset Grant, though. He laughed and told the man to get off his bike before he decides to take pictures.

5 What was Grant doing when the man fell onto him?
A riding a bike **B** walking
C taking a picture

2 Read the articles again and match the headings with each article.

1 Not Safe at Sea ___
2 A Moving Picture ___
3 A Bad Phone Call ___
4 One Morning, Three Accidents ___
5 Asleep at the Wheel ___

Wordpower!

3 Choose the correct word.

1 Sarah was **upset / successful** about the accident she had yesterday.
2 Michael **knocked / got out** a bicycle when he was walking to work the other day.
3 Lisa had a car **escape / crash** this morning, but it wasn't serious.
4 I'm trying to **knock / get out** of the car, but the door won't open!
5 Donna left her small town and became a(n) **extremely / successful** singer.
6 That car almost hit you! You're **successful / lucky** you didn't get hurt.
7 She didn't want to talk to Tom, so she made her **crash / escape** through the back of the café.
8 It's **lucky / extremely** difficult to drive in the snow.

4 Write a word from the box in each gap.

crash • escape • extremely • getting out • knocked • lucky • successful • upset

Francis: Kevin, are you OK? I heard about your car (1) __________ .
Kevin: I'm fine, Francis, thanks. It wasn't serious. I was really (2) __________ .
Francis: That's good. I was (3) __________ when I heard about it. What happened?
Kevin: I was driving home from work when I saw Louis Porter (4) __________ of his car.
Francis: Louis Porter? I've heard that name. Is he a (5) __________ baseball player?
Kevin: Yes! I stopped the car when I saw him, but another car hit me. The driver (6) __________ my car into the middle of the street, then he left!
Francis: Did he ask you if you were OK?
Kevin: No! It seems he wanted to make a quick (7) __________ . I was (8) __________ angry about that, but I got to meet Louis Porter, and I wasn't hurt.

Grammar 1 G

Past continuous

Look again at *Grammar database 15* on page 151 before doing these exercises.

1 Write a verb from the box in each gap. Use the past continuous.

cook • drive • laugh • not play • not travel • ride • sail • watch

1 They __________ *The Great Escape* on TV last night.
2 She __________ her bike really fast down the street.
3 Ralph __________ in his boat when the storm came.
4 I called you yesterday but you __________ dinner.
5 We __________ by bus on the day of the accident – we were walking.
6 I __________ really hard at the funny joke.
7 They __________ Sam's car into the mountains.
8 We __________ football yesterday because it was very hot.

2 Choose the correct word or phrase.

1 She **got / was getting** out of the car when the driver stopped.
2 They **were filming / filmed** the sleeping lion when it woke up.
3 Kyle and Mark **fished / were fishing** when Mark fell out of the boat.
4 The dog jumped off the table when Mary **came / was coming** into the room.
5 George **drove / was driving** to work when he saw a bad crash.
6 The driver made a mistake and **was turning / turned** down the wrong street.

3 Tick (✔) the correct sentences. Underline the mistake in the incorrect sentences and write the correct word or phrase.

1 The kids played in the park when it started to rain. ___ ___________
2 Jill was answering the phone when it began to ring. ___ ___________
3 The fans were taking pictures while the singer was signing autographs. ___ ___________
4 Jake rode his bike when he hit the tree. ___ ___________
5 Did Linda scream when she was seeing the dangerous animal? ___ ___________
6 Ryan ran down the field when Martin jumped on him and knocked him down. ___ ___________

4 Read the text and for each question, choose the correct answer, A, B or C.

Our holiday last week was great, but we had quite a scary time one day. We (1) ___ through the mountains and enjoying the day when my dad (2) ___ something very strange in the middle of the road. He (3) ___ the car in front of it because we weren't able to drive around it. While he (4) ___ out of the car, the thing in the road started to move. It was a great big bear! I think it (5) ___ in the middle of the road when we arrived. My dad (6) ___ back into the car when he saw it move. The bear stood up, (7) ___ over to our car and looked right at us. I was so scared! Then my mum (8) ___ to give the bear our sandwiches. She (9) ___ them out of the window as far as she could, and while the bear (10) ___ to get them, we left! I'm so glad we had some food with us, or we would still be on the mountain in the car!

1 **A** was driving **B** were driving **C** drove
2 **A** seeing **B** was seeing **C** saw
3 **A** was stopping **B** stopped **C** were stopping
4 **A** get **B** got **C** was getting
5 **A** was sleeping **B** slept **C** sleeping
6 **A** was getting **B** were getting **C** got
7 **A** walked **B** was walking **C** walking
8 **A** was decided **B** decided **C** was deciding
9 **A** was throwing **B** throws **C** threw
10 **A** runs **B** was running **C** ran

Wordpower!

1 Write a letter in each gap to complete the words or phrases. The first letter is given to help you.

1 This is something two people do with their hands when they meet or say goodbye. **s** ___ ___ ___ ___
2 This is something you do with your head when you mean 'yes'. **n** ___ ___
3 This is something you do with your mouth to show that you love someone. **k** ___ ___ ___
4 This is something you do with your hand when you want to say 'hi' to someone who is far away. **w** ___ ___ ___
5 This is something you do with your finger when you want to show something to someone. **p** ___ ___ ___ ___
6 This is something you do when your move your head quickly from side to side. **s** ___ ___ ___ ___

2 Use words from Exercise 1 in the correct form to complete the dialogue.

Jimmy: You'll never get a taxi in this rainy weather, Fran!
Fran: Don't worry. I'll put my hand up and (1) ____________ at one of them.
Jimmy: There's one right there! Oh, no. Never mind. He's (2) ____________ his head. He's not stopping.
Fran: What if we move to another street? There are taxis over there. Do you see where I'm (3) ____________ with my finger?
Jimmy: Wait, I think this taxi will stop. Yes, he's (4) ____________ his head.
Fran: I'm so glad. It's really raining now!
Jimmy: OK, well, let's (5) ____________ hands before you leave.
Fran: Oh, come on, Jimmy! We know each other better! (6) ____________ me on the cheek and I'll be on my way …

Listening

CD Track 10

1 Listen to two teenagers talking and decide if these statements are true (T) or false (F).

1 Trevor was travelling on a train with his mum and dad. T/F
2 Trevor learned about his lucky escape while he was reading the news. T/F
3 Monica was travelling on a boat that was returning to England. T/F
4 Monica felt sick after her mum said she saw land. T/F
5 Monica's boat trip was only 15 minutes long. T/F
6 Trevor thought Monica's boat trip seemed exciting. T/F

CD Track 10

2 Listen to the conversation again and complete the gaps.

1 Trevor was travelling on a train through ____________ .
2 Trevor got off the train and stayed in a town for one ____________ .
3 Monica was travelling with her mum and ____________ during her lucky escape.
4 Monica's mum saw land from the ____________ of the boat.
5 Monica now thinks the boat ride was ____________ .
6 Monica says she will only travel by boat again if the ____________ is shining.

Grammar 2 G

Short answer forms

Look again at *Grammar database 16* on page 151 before doing these exercises.

1 Each of the words in bold is incorrect. Write the correct words on the lines.

1 Were you walking home when you saw the crash?
Yes, I **were**. ____________

2 Did Martin see the accident?
No, he **wasn't**. ____________

3 Can you call the police right now?
Yes, I **am**. ____________

4 Was he talking on the phone when he dropped it down the hole?
No, he **didn't**. ____________

5 I heard you fell off your bike. Are you OK?
Yes, I **was**. ____________

6 Did you tell your mum what happened?
Yes, I **told**. ____________

7 Were they sitting in the park when it started to rain?
No, they **wasn't**. ____________

8 Have you got the number for Stanley's parents?
Yes, I **do**. ____________

2 Answer the questions with short answers. *Yes* for (✔) and *No* for (✘).

1 Did you meet the famous singer? (✔) ____________
2 Was she signing autographs? (✔) ____________
3 Were you able to get an autograph? (✔) ____________
4 Are you going to her concert tonight? (✘) ____________
5 Can we go for a walk in the park? (✔) ____________
6 Do you think that it will rain? (✔) ____________
7 Have you got an umbrella? (✘) ____________
8 Should we buy one on the way to the park? (✘) ____________

3 Write a word in each gap to complete the dialogue.

Evan: (1) ____________ you talking to David yesterday when I called you?
Sue: Yes, I (2) ____________. Did you know he went on a trip to South Africa?
Evan: No, (3) ____________ didn't! Did he tell you how it went?
Sue: Yes, (4) ____________ did. He said it was amazing. He took a boat trip with his parents while he (5) ____________ staying there and they saw a huge whale. Can you believe it?
Evan: No, I (6) ____________! How did they see it?
Sue: They (7) ____________ sailing in the ocean and it just jumped out of the water.
Evan: Did David get a picture of it?
Sue: No, he (8) ____________! But he was happy that he saw a whale for the first time. Are there whales near England?
Evan: Yes, (9) ____________ are! There was one in London actually. It (10) ____________ swimming in the River Thames.
Sue: Wow!

Quick check

4 Choose the correct answer.

1 Do we use the past continuous to show that something was in progress when something else happened? **yes / no**
2 Can we use the past continuous with the past simple in the same sentence? **yes / no**
3 Which is correct? **She was working when I called. / She worked when I called. / both**
4 Do we use short answers when we want to give a polite answer? **yes / no**
5 Do we always put the main verb of a question in the short answer? **yes / no**
6 Which answer is correct for this question: Do we have to go now?
Yes, we do. / Yes, we have. / both

Writing

1 Read the story and put the events in order.

Last weekend, my friends and I decided to visit the city zoo. My friend Marcy was taking pictures. When we were near the elephants, something really funny happened.

One of the elephants was standing near the front. Marcy told us to stand in front of it so she could take a picture. We walked over to the elephant and turned toward Marcy. Marcy got ready to take the picture.

Then something scary happened. Marcy was looking through her camera when the elephant made a really loud sound. My friend Jessica started to scream! We moved away from the elephant very quickly.

Later we looked at the picture. Both the elephant's and Jessica's mouths were wide open! It was a great picture and I laughed really hard!

1 The writer and her friends stood in front of an elephant. ___
2 One of the writer's friends screamed. ___
3 The writer and her friends were looking at pictures. ___
4 Marcy got ready to take a picture of her friends. ___
5 The writer and her friends visited the elephants. ___
6 The writer decided to visit the zoo with friends. _1_

2 Read the story again and choose the correct word or phrase.

1 This story happened **during the week / at the weekend**.
2 The **writer / writer's friend** was taking pictures of animals.
3 The elephant in the photo was standing **close to the front / far away**.
4 **Marcy / Jessica** screamed when the elephant made a loud sound.
5 **Only the writer / The writer and her friends** moved away from the elephant.
6 The writer thought the picture was **scary / funny**.

Check your progress! | Units 7-8

1 Choose the correct word or phrase.

Airports can be difficult. I travelled to Rome with my family last month. I was very excited when the plane (1) **landed / took off** in Rome but after we got inside the airport, I was quite angry and (2) **successful / upset**. We got off the plane and the security guard checked my (3) **baggage / passport**. He looked at the photo and he started to (4) **shake / wave** his head. He didn't think it was me! I was (5) **upset / lucky** because my dad was there to talk to him. The security guard let me go, so we got our (6) **baggage / passenger** and left. After our holiday was over, we had another problem at the airport. They put my bags through the scanner and they saw sharp (7) **metal / cotton** objects inside. They said the objects could hurt another (8) **emergency / passenger** on the plane, and I had to leave them! I was (9) **extremely / lucky** sad as these were the gifts for my friends! I was glad when the plane (10) **took off / landed** and we left for home. I had fun in Rome, but I didn't like the airport at all!

10 marks

2 Put the verbs into the past simple or past continuous.

My friend Jason and I (11) ____________ (**walk**) through the city centre the other day when we (12) ____________ (**see**) a strange accident. A man (13) ____________ (**drive**) his car down a busy street when a woman suddenly (14) ____________ (**run**) in front of his car. The man (15) ____________ (**not have**) time to stop and he (16) ____________ (**hit**) the woman. The woman was lucky because the man (17) ____________ (**not go**) very fast when he (18) ____________ (**knock**) her down. She wasn't hurt and they both felt sorry.

8 marks

3 For each question, choose the correct answer, A, B or C.

19 You can't go in there, Paul. That bathroom is for ___ only.

A woman **B** women **C** womans

20 I really like the ___ they play in this club.

A musics **B** musices **C** music

21 I asked my dad for ___ advice on a problem I had at school.

A any **B** much **C** some

22 There are ___ flights from London to New York every day.

A much **B** a lot **C** many

23 I'm sorry, but there are ___ rooms left at this hotel.

A no **B** any **C** much

24 'Can I see your new shoes? 'Yes, you ___.'

A see **B** can **C** are

25 'Were you working when she called?' 'No, I ___.'

A haven't **B** didn't **C** wasn't

7 marks

Total:___ / 25 marks

9

Friends and Family!

Reading

1 Read the texts and for each question, choose the correct answer, A or B.

1 The two texts are …
A articles.
B emails.

2 ___ wants her friend's help.
A Vera
B Andrea

3 Andrea is ___ right now.
A upset
B angry

2 Write *yes* or *no* to answer each question.

1 Did Andrea write to Vera yesterday?
___

2 Do we know where Andrea is right now?
___

3 Is Andrea's party on Monday?
___

4 Do we know why Andrea is having a party?
___

5 Did Vera's mother give her permission to go to the party?
___

6 Did Vera cry when she was talking to her mother?
___

7 Does Vera's mum think she is too young to do some things?
___

8 Does Andrea know Vera's mum?
___

9 Do we know what Andrea's relationship with her parents is?
___

10 Does Andrea give Vera advice?
___

write reply send

Hi, Andrea,
Thanks for your email yesterday – I'm happy you're enjoying yourself at your grandmother's in the countryside. I'm not enjoying myself. I am extremely angry at the moment! On Monday, I told my mum about your party on Friday, May 18th and she said I can't go! I almost cried when she didn't give me permission. My mother never lets me do the things I want to. Never! It's not fair. I argued with her, but she said no. When will she let me grow up? I *cannot* get on with her because she doesn't understand me. And she doesn't trust me. I don't know what to do.
Any advice?
Write soon,
Vera

write reply send

Hello, Vera,
I was very upset when I read your email this morning. I'm sad that you're having problems with your mum. She always seems so nice when I talk to her. Perhaps you have to try and see things from her side. She worries about you, so she doesn't allow you to do some things. Remember that to her, you're her little girl! I have an idea, though. I hope it helps. Try not to argue with her and never shout! You have to show her that you're old enough to do things like go to parties and out with your friends. Perhaps you can ask your dad to drive you to my party and then home again. I think your mum might say yes to this arrangement – you can ask. Write back and tell me what happens. Good luck!
Andrea

Wordpower!

3 Each of the words in bold is in the wrong sentence. Write a word in bold from another sentence to replace the incorrect one.

1 I want to come, but I need my dad to **get** his permission first. ________
2 They said I can't go. It's not **relationship**! ________
3 Her parents trust her, so they **grow** her do what she wants. ________
4 Don't **allow** with me, Tarek. I said no! ________
5 Can you believe his parents don't **argue** him to go to parties? ________
6 **Let** up, Benny! Why can't you be more mature? ________
7 I **give** on with Bach and Hans, but Greta is my best friend. ________
8 Georgia has got a very close **fair** with her family. ________

4 Write a word from the box in each gap.

allow • argue • fair • get • grow • let • permission • relationship

Lauren: Wow! You look really angry, Izza. What happened?
Izza: I'm very upset right now, Lauren. My parents won't (1) ________ me go to the school party on Friday night!
Lauren: Oh, no! That's very bad news. Why didn't they give you (2) ________ ?
Izza: Because they don't want me to (3) ________ up. I'm not seven years old! It's not (4) ________ !
Lauren: Perhaps you have to see your (5) ________ from their side.
Izza: What do you mean, Lauren? I try to (6) ________ on with them, but they never listen.
Lauren: Do you get upset when you talk to them? Do you shout?
Izza: Yes, but ...
Lauren: Try not to (7) ________ with them. Try to smile and explain how you feel without getting angry.
Izza: Hmm, that might help.
Lauren: Yes, and then perhaps they'll (8) ________ you to go to the school party.

Grammar 1

G

can **and** ***could***

Look again at *Grammar database 17* on page 152 before doing these exercises.

1 Tick (✔) the correct sentences.

1 I could go to the park with you tomorrow. Mum said no. ☐
2 Ms Thomas, could I take this book home, please? ☐
3 Can you help me with this please, Mr Riggs? ☐
4 She can't feed the dog because she was at school. ☐
5 My brother can talk until he was two years old. Now he never stops! ☐
6 You can go to the party, but be home at ten. ☐
7 My dad can speak Polish, but he couldn't speak German. ☐
8 Hey, Troy, could I use your laptop? ☐
9 No, you cannot use my video game! ☐
10 When I was six, I could to read and write. ☐

2 Complete the gaps in the sentences with *can, can't, could* or *couldn't*.

1 Hey, Mum, __________ I have some money?
2 You __________ go until you do all your homework.
3 Mr Rogers, __________ I talk to you, please?
4 Stephan __________ speak English until last year.
5 Sally __________ come with us. Her parents gave their permission.
6 Bach __________ go to the concert. His parents won't let him.
7 He __________ talk to you right now. He's busy.
8 __________ you drive me to Sean's house, Dad?
9 I __________ get on with that new girl! She's nasty and rude.
10 __________ you please stop talking, Peter?

3 Rewrite to make questions and negative sentences.

1 I can go to the party tonight.
Can I go to the party tonight? *I can't go to the party tonight.*
2 Ivan could speak three languages when he was five.
__________ __________
3 We could help you with that.
__________ __________
4 They can take us to the restaurant.
__________ __________
5 You could come with us.
__________ __________
6 Marta can drive a car.
__________ __________

4 Answer the questions in Exercise 3 using short answers.

1 No, __________. 3 Yes, __________. 5 No, __________.
2 Yes, __________. 4 No, __________. 6 Yes, __________.

Wordpower!

1 Rewrite the words to complete the gaps in the sentences.

1 Jacques is frowning because he's ____________ (**tupes**) about his friend.
2 She's ____________ (**naygr**) because her parents won't give her permission to go to the play.
3 My parents are ____________ (**rredowi**) that I might fall and get hurt.
4 Were you ____________ (**drispruse**) that Wendy could speak Russian?
5 Paul said Tori was coming, but Sade said Tori wasn't coming; I'm very ____________ (**desufnoc**)!
6 Don't be ____________ (**racsde**). It's just a film!

2 Write a word in each gap to complete the text. The first letter is given to help you.

Relationships can often be difficult. However, always remember that no-one gets on well with all their family or all their friends all the time. There are days when we get (1) **a**____________ because our mum or our dad doesn't give us permission to do something, days when we are (2) **u**____________ because life doesn't seem fair. There are days when we feel (3) **c**____________ because a friend isn't talking to us, but we don't know what we did. Don't be sad about things like that. And don't be (4) **s**____________ that you'll lose your friend. You might be (5) **s**____________ to learn that talking to people without shouting, without crying, and without arguing can make things better immediately. So, when you are (6) **w**____________ because you have a problem with your parents or your best friend, sit down and talk to them. You'll be happy you did!

Listening

CD Track 11

1 Listen to the conversation between a mother and her child and decide if these statements are true (T) or false (F).

1 Layla is talking to her mother on Monday. T/F
2 Layla doesn't look happy. T/F
3 Layla asks for her mother's permission. T/F
4 Layla goes swimming once a week. T/F
5 Susan has got a small house. T/F
6 Susan's party is on a school night. T/F
7 Susan is nearly 14 years old. T/F
8 Layla wants her mum to buy some new clothes. T/F

CD Track 11

2 Listen again and complete the gaps.

PLEASE COME!

What: Susan's birthday (1) __________ !

When: Saturday, (2) __________ 12th

Where: (3) __________ Restaurant

(4) 24 __________ Road

Time: 7pm to (5) __________

FOOD, MUSIC and FUN!

Grammar 2

should, must* and *have to

Look again at *Grammar database 18* on page 152 before doing these exercises.

1 **Put a line through the incorrect sentences.**

1 I shouldn't to go to the cinema. / I shouldn't go to the cinema.
2 *Does he have to go?* No, he mustn't. / No, he doesn't.
3 We doesn't must get tickets. / We don't have to get tickets.
4 You shouldn't shout all the time. / You not should shout all the time.
5 *Do I have to do the washing up, Mum?* No, you shouldn't. / Yes, you do.
6 *What's the matter, Mr Robbins?* You have to try harder. / You must to try harder.
7 *Does Stella have to do her homework?* Yes, she has. / Yes, she does.
8 You can come to the party, but you don't have to. / You can come to the party, but you mustn't.

2 **Put the words into the correct order to make sentences or questions.**

1 have / after / look / your / Do / to / you / brother? / little
Do you have to look after your little brother?
2 room. / don't / have / We / our / clean / to
____
3 mustn't / cry. / You
____
4 to / Your / talk / must / you. / friend
____
5 I / teacher? / Should / ask / the
____
6 to / has / bins. / the / empty / Sophia
____
7 permission. / to / We / for / ask / have
____
8 shouldn't / You / angry. / get
____
9 say / you're / You / sorry. / should
____
10 to / We / promise / help. / must
____

3 **Match 1–5 with a–h. There are three letters you do not need to use.**

1 You mustn't swim here. ___
2 You have to be a pupil to go on the trip. ___
3 You shouldn't run here. ___
4 You don't have to buy a ticket. ___
5 You shouldn't swim after eating. ___

a Only pupils should run here.
b It's never a good idea to eat and then swim!
c Pupils must have a ticket.
d Be careful. It's not safe to run here.
e Pupils only!
f No swimming!
g Come in! No cost!
h All pupils welcome.

Quick check

4 **Choose the correct answer.**

1 Do we use *can* and *could* to talk about ability and make requests? **yes / no**
2 Do *can't* and *cannot* mean the same thing? **yes / no**
3 Which one is correct? **Could you to talk to her? / Could you talk to her? / both**
4 Which one is correct? **You can't go. / You cannot to go. / both**
5 Do *mustn't* and *don't have to* mean the same thing? **yes / no**
6 Do *must* and *have to* mean different things? **yes / no**
7 For the short answers, do we use the same modal as in the questions? **yes / no**
8 After *can*, *could*, *should*, *must* and *have to*, do we use the bare infinitive? **yes / no**

Writing

1 **Read the text and underline all the modals.**

THE PHELPS FAMILY RULES

All of us have to help around the house. Yes, that means you too, Frannie! Duke, you don't have to help because you're a dog.

On Mondays, Wednesdays and Fridays, Frannie has to do the washing up and Hans has to empty the bins. Hans, you mustn't forget the bin in your room!

Mum must cook lunch and dinner on Saturdays and Sundays. Dad must cook dinner on weekdays. He can buy pizzas on really busy days.

Hans has to feed Duke every morning and give him water. Frannie has to feed him every night. She should do it before 6pm or he gets upset. Hans, could you feed Duke for Frannie on the days she gets back late from football matches, please?

These are the new rules. I couldn't think of any others. You can talk to me or Mum about them. You shouldn't shout or cry when you talk to us about them. Be mature – we can solve any problems together!

2 **Complete the table with modals from Exercise 1.**

present/past ability	give permission	make polite requests	obligation	lack of obligation	give advice
(1)	(2)	(5)	(6)	(14)	(15)
	(3)		(7)		(16)
	(4)		(8)		
			(9)		
			(10)		
			(11)		
			(12)		
			(13)		

10

Being the Best!

Reading

1 **Read the statements and for each question, choose the correct answer, A, B or C.**

http://www.kidscorner.co.uk

Home | News | School stuff | Stories

Kids' Corner

Kids' stories teach us important lessons. Read these books and learn to live better!

- **Green Eggs and Ham by Dr Seuss**
  A character named Sam tries to get another character to eat green food. Sam asks if he would eat it in a boat or a house, or with a goat or a mouse! The other character doesn't want to eat the strange food, but he eventually agrees to do it if Sam leaves him alone. After he tries the food, he decides he likes it. The story tells kids that you can't know you don't like something until you try it.

- **The Little Engine that Could**
  This is a story about a small train, or 'engine', that pulls a very large train over a mountain. There are other trains that are bigger than the small train, but they don't want to do it because they worry that the job is too difficult. The small train decides to do it. While he pulls the train, he says 'I think I can, I think I can.' And he does! The story teaches children that some jobs may seem difficult, but that doesn't mean they can't do them.

- **Aesop's fable**
  The Boy who Cried Wolf
  A boy decides to play a game with the people of his village. He shouts that he sees a wolf – an animal that's like a dog but more dangerous – that's trying to eat the farmers' sheep. The villagers run to see the wolf, but the wolf isn't there. The boy does it again and the villagers come, but there's no wolf. In the end, a wolf really comes, the boy screams, but no-one comes and the wolf eats the sheep. The lesson is if you lie too much, no-one will believe you when you tell the truth.

1 In the first story, the character doesn't want to eat the food because it looks funny.
A Right **B** Wrong **C** Doesn't say

2 The food in the first story is a green goat and a green mouse.
A Right **B** Wrong **C** Doesn't say

3 Sam likes the food that he's trying to get the other character to eat.
A Right **B** Wrong **C** Doesn't say

4 In the second story, the other trains are afraid to pull the very large train.
A Right **B** Wrong **C** Doesn't say

5 When the small train pulls the large train, the large train says something over and over again.
A Right **B** Wrong **C** Doesn't say

6 In the last story, the boy tells the villagers that he sees sheep trying to run away.
A Right **B** Wrong **C** Doesn't say

7 A wolf eventually comes to the place where the boy is.
A Right **B** Wrong **C** Doesn't say

8 The villagers believe the boy every single time he says there's a wolf.
A Right **B** Wrong **C** Doesn't say

Wordpower!

2 Each of the words in bold is in the wrong sentence. Write a word in bold from another sentence to replace the incorrect one.

1 The last runner isn't at the finish line yet, but he'll be here **by mistake**. ______
2 I know the answer to this question. I'm **competition** of it! ______
3 A race is a kind of **right** that only one person can win. ______
4 My sister **gives up** with me … we both think winning is great! ______
5 When Paul tries a new sport, he always **agrees** something wonderful about it. ______
6 I wasn't trying to win … I won **eventually**! ______
7 If Michelle isn't doing well at something, she just **discovers**! ______
8 You were **certain** and I was wrong … Tom won the race, not Mark. ______

3 Write a word or phrase from the box in each gap.

agree • by mistake • certain • competition • discover • eventually • give up • right

My dad is always telling me to do my best. If I am in a (1) ______, such as a race at school, he tells me to keep trying to do better. I know he's (2) ______, too. I practise for hours after school and at the weekend. I get tired, but my dad tells me not to (3) ______, even when I'm tired. Then I (4) ______ things that I didn't know before. I can run very fast, even when I'm tired! He tells me to practise every day, and (5) ______ I will be a very fast runner. I have a race in two weeks, and I'm (6) ______ that I can win. My friends (7) ______ with me, because they watch me and they see how fast I can run. I'm sure that if someone else wins this race, it will be (8) ______!

Grammar 1

G

Comparatives

Look again at *Grammar database 19* on page 153 before doing these exercises.

1 Complete the sentences using the comparative.

1 Frank is ______ (**good**) at running than Charlie.
2 An ox is a lot ______ (**strong**) than a donkey.
3 Donna's sister is ______ (**tall**) than her.
4 The moon is ______ (**small**) than the Sun.
5 Ronald says that lions are ______ (**interesting**) than mice.
6 My cat is ______ (**large**) than my dog!
7 This sofa is ______ (**comfortable**) than that plastic chair.
8 My twin brother is a few minutes ______ (**young**) than me.

2 Look at the pictures and complete the sentences with an adjective from the box in the comparative.

cold • difficult • easy • fast • happy • hot • sad • slow

1 The hare is ____________ than the tortoise and the tortoise is ____________ than the hare.
2 The lion is ____________ than the mouse and the mouse is ____________ than the lion.
3 The ox's job is ____________ than the frog's and the frog's job is ____________ than the ox's.
4 The North Wind is ____________ than the Sun and the Sun is ____________ than the North Wind.

1

2

3

4

3 Choose the correct word or phrase.

My brother Ryan and I sometimes play games with each other to see which one of us is (1) **more quick / quicker** at doing something. For example, when Mum tells us to clean our rooms, I try to clean my room (2) **faster / more fast** than Ryan. And with homework, I try to do mine in a (3) **more short / shorter** amount of time than Ryan. Sometimes I win, and sometimes he wins. But I know this to be true: the winner isn't always (4) **better / more good** than the loser. If I finish cleaning my room first, Ryan's room is always (5) **more clean / cleaner** than mine. If Ryan finishes his homework first, my handwriting always looks (6) **nicer / more nice** than his. So, it may be (7) **enjoyabler / more enjoyable** to win a race, but it's (8) **more smart / smarter** to take your time doing things than to do them really fast so you can win!

4 Write sentences using the comparative.

1 My dad / old / my mum
My dad is older than my mum.

2 A mouse / weak / an elephant
____

3 Maths / not hard / history
____

4 Running / boring / swimming
____

5 A lion / scary / mouse
____

6 Stephen / angry / George
____

Wordpower!

1 Choose the correct word.

1 This box is very **heavy / light**. I can't move it!
2 My sister is a model and she's quite tall and **heavy / thin**.
3 My cat Oscar eats a lot and now he's **fat / light**!
4 Henry has got **dark / slim** hair and green eyes.
5 Michelle's hair gets very **light / dark** in the summer.
6 Bill is quite **slim / fat** because he runs a lot.
7 Sarah's got blue eyes and **fair / slim** hair.
8 This bicycle is very **heavy / light**, so it's easy to carry.

2 Read the text and for each question, choose the correct answer, A, B or C.

Martin: It's strange that family members can be so different.

Jessica: I know. My sister's hair is (1) ___ than mine. My mum's hair is (2) ___ than mine and Dad's hair is a lot (3) ___ than my mum's! See, we're all different!

Martin: Well, everyone in my family has the same hair colour – brown! But we're not all the same size. My brother Jason plays sport all the time, so he's a lot (4) ___ than me. My brother Nick, though, eats all the time, so he's (5) ___ than me!

Jessica: Ha, ha! Well, I'm not (6) ___ than my sister. We're the same size.

Martin: I think my brother Nick needs to play sport. Then he'll be (7) ___ than he is now.

Jessica: That's a good idea. Running is good for that. After a few weeks of it, he'll probably be (8) ___ than you!

1 **A** heavier **B** lighter **C** slimmer
2 **A** slimmer **B** fatter **C** darker
3 **A** darker **B** heavier **C** fatter
4 **A** slimmer **B** fatter **C** heavier
5 **A** thinner **B** fatter **C** slimmer
6 **A** fairer **B** darker **C** heavier
7 **A** heavier **B** thinner **C** fatter
8 **A** lighter **B** fatter **C** heavier

Listening

CD Track 12

1 Listen to part of a conversation and for each question, choose the correct answer, A, B or C.

1 Danielle and Jeffrey are talking about …
A school. **B** free time. **C** sport.
2 Danielle and Jeffrey agree on …
A some things. **B** everything. **C** nothing.
3 Jeffrey thinks a subject is important if we …
A like it. **B** use it a lot. **C** know a lot about it.
4 Danielle thinks subjects we use often in life aren't always …
A boring. **B** interesting. **C** important.

CD Track 13

2 Listen to the complete conversation and choose the correct word or phrase.

1 Danielle says that history is **more important / more interesting** than maths.
2 Jeffrey **agrees / doesn't agree** with what Danielle says about history and maths.
3 Danielle thinks that maths is **more boring / more interesting** than science.
4 **Maths / Science** is the subject that Jeffrey likes the most.
5 Danielle thinks it's more fun to study **history / English**.
6 Jeffrey thinks we use **maths and science / English and history** more often.

Grammar 2 G

Superlatives

Look again at *Grammar database 20* on page 153 before doing these exercises.

1 Each of the words or phrases in bold is incorrect. Write the correct words on the lines.

1 I think skiing is the most **danger** sport in the world. ____________
2 Our teacher is the **tall** person in our classroom. ____________
3 I'm so happy! I got the **higher** mark in my class! ____________
4 Mike won the race. He's the **more fast** runner in school! ____________
5 I don't enjoy maths. It's the **bad** subject. ____________
6 I think David Beckham is the **good** player in football. ____________

2 Write sentences or questions using the superlative.

1 Eric / slim person / in my family

____

2 Mary / long hair / in school

____

3 Basketball / enjoyable / sport

____

4 Which chair / comfortable chair / in your house?

____

5 Elephants / heavy animals / in this zoo

____

6 Chess / interesting game / in the world

____

3 Read the text and for each question, choose the correct answer, A, B or C.

What's the world's (1) ___ bridge? This title goes to the Millau Viaduct in France, a bridge for cars that's 343 metres (2) ___ . The bridge is very (3) ___ and it even looks like it's sitting in the sky. Which bridge is the (4) ___ bridge in the world? One very (5) ___ bridge is the Pons Fabricius in Rome, made in 63 BC. It's not a very (6) ___ bridge, at about 60 metres, and it's not very (7) ___ , at about 6 metres, but it travels across the Tiber River in the centre of Rome and it's still very much in use today. There are bridges in the world that are (8) ___ than the Pons Fabricius, such as bridges in Greece from 1600 BC, but they're not in use any more. They are also much (9) ___ than the Pons Fabricius. And the (10) ___ bridge in the world? Some say this is the Golden Gate Bridge in San Francisco. Other people say Tower Bridge in London is (11) ___ than the Golden Gate. Most agree that both bridges are (12) ___ in their own way.

	A	B	C
1	**A** taller	**B** most tall	**C** tallest
2	**A** tallest	**B** tall	**C** taller
3	**A** highest	**B** higher	**C** high
4	**A** oldest	**B** most old	**C** old
5	**A** older	**B** more old	**C** old
6	**A** longest	**B** long	**C** longer
7	**A** wide	**B** wider	**C** widest
8	**A** more old	**B** older	**C** oldest
9	**A** more small	**B** small	**C** smaller
10	**A** famous	**B** most famous	**C** more famous
11	**A** most famous	**B** famous	**C** more famous
12	**A** beautiful	**B** more beautiful	**C** most beautiful

Quick check

4 Choose the correct answer.

1 Do we use comparatives to talk about things that are the same? **yes / no**
2 Do we always use *than* when we use comparatives? **yes / no**
3 Which is correct? **That's the better book. / That book's better than this one. / both**
4 Do we use superlatives to compare one thing with other things in the same group? **yes / no**
5 Do we usually put *the* before the superlative? **yes / no**
6 Which is correct? **That's the best ice cream! / That's the best! / both**

Writing

1 Read the description, then tick (✔) the things that are mentioned and cross (X) the things that are not mentioned.

I'm Karen, and I've got quite a big family! My dad and mum are Joseph and Linda, and I've got three brothers, Jake, Barnie and Louis. Mum and I are the only girls in the family! My mum is not as tall as my dad, but she's only a bit shorter than him. My brother Jake is the tallest person in my family. He's even taller than my dad! Barnie and Louis are both shorter than me, but they're also a lot younger than me, so that makes sense!

Both my dad and my mum have got short brown hair, but my mum's hair is longer than my dad's. Jake and Barnie's hair is fairer than my mum's and dad's hair, but Louis and I have got the same hair colour – brown, just like Mum and Dad.

All of us are thin, but Barnie and Louis are the thinnest, but they're only nine and seven years old. I'm fourteen, Jake's nineteen, and Mum and Dad, well, they're the oldest! I think as you get older, you're not as slim as you once were. My parents keep fit though, and they tell us to keep fit as well. Well, that's my family!

1 The number of people in Karen's family. ___
2 How tall Karen's family members are. ___
3 What Karen's family members like to wear. ___
4 What kind of hair Karen's family members have got. ___
5 What Karen's family members like to do at the weekend. ___
6 Who the youngest members of Karen's family are. ___
7 How big Karen's family members are. ___
8 What Karen thinks about getting older. ___

2 Rewrite the sentences using *not as* + adjective + *as*.

1 Bill is fat, but John is fatter.
Bill is not as fat as John.
2 Lisa is fast, but Nicole is faster.
______
3 Maths is interesting, but history is more interesting.
______
4 Basketball is hard, but football is not hard.
______
5 Mrs Johnson is nice, but Mr Peters is not nice.
______
6 The sofa is comfortable, but the chair is not comfortable.
______

Check your progress! | Units 9-10

1 Write a word in each gap to complete the sentences. The first letter is given to help you.

1 I want to come, but my Mum needs to give me **p** __ __ __ __ __ __ __ __ __ first.

2 Maggie's parents don't **a** __ __ __ __ her to go out on school nights.

3 Stephen is **w** __ __ __ __ __ __ that he won't win the race on Saturday.

4 I am **c** __ __ __ __ __ __ Philip did his best.

5 She's the most beautiful girl in the class. Look at her **d** __ __ __ hair and blue eyes.

6 Eventually, my brother won the singing **c** __ __ __ __ __ __ __ __ __ __.

7 The chess player with the **f** __ __ __ hair is the best in the world.

7 marks

2 Write a word or phrase in each gap to complete the sentences.

8 **A:** Is a cheetah ________ **(fastest / faster)** than a hare?
B: I don't know. But I'm certain a hare is ________ **(the quickest / quicker)** than a tortoise.

9 **A:** Sally, ________ **(must / could)** I use your computer, please?
B: Of course you ________ **(can / should)**, Jason.

10 **A:** You ________ **(shouldn't / can't)** argue with your brother.
B: I know, but he is ________ **(rudest / the rudest)** person in the world!

11 **A:** Peter, you ________ **(must / can)** do your homework before you go out.
B: Oh, Dad, do I ________ **(have to / has to)**?

8 marks

3 Read the text and for each question, choose the correct answer, A, B or C.

BEING THE BEST YOU CAN BE

I love my sister, I really do, but sometimes she makes me so angry. She's (12) ___ than me, she's (13) ___ than me and she works (14) ___ in school than me – it's just not fair! And to make things worse, she's a really lovely girl! Yesterday, she bought a new pair of shoes. I said to her, '(15) ___ I wear your new shoes to Tim's party tonight?' I (16) ___ believe it, but she said, 'Of course you (17) ___, Jan. You know you (18) ___ have to ask me when you want to wear my things.' She makes me want to scream. I told my best friend Emily about it and she said, 'I'm confused. Why does having (19) ___ nicest sister in the world upset you? You (20) ___ be happy about it.' I thought about it for a bit and eventually I said to Emily, 'You're right. I (21) ___ stop being jealous of her, and just be the best I can be.'

	A	B	C
12	old	older	oldest
13	slimmer	more slimmer	most slimmer
14	hard	hardest	harder
15	Must	Couldn't	Could
16	couldn't	mustn't	shouldn't
17	must	can	have to
18	shouldn't	don't	mustn't
19	the	a	an
20	can	could	should
21	must	can't	shouldn't

10 marks

Total: ____ / 25 marks

11

Planning for Tomorrow!

Reading

1 Read the article and for each question, choose the correct answer, A, B or C.

1 Wafi lives in a big house in Cairo.
A Right **B** Wrong **C** Doesn't say

2 Wafi goes to a sports school now.
A Right **B** Wrong **C** Doesn't say

3 Wafi is a bit worried about his first game.
A Right **B** Wrong **C** Doesn't say

4 Sylvia is older than Wafi.
A Right **B** Wrong **C** Doesn't say

5 Sylvia knows what drama school she is going to go to.
A Right **B** Wrong **C** Doesn't say

6 Sylvia thinks she'll have a husband some day.
A Right **B** Wrong **C** Doesn't say

7 Asad studies languages at school.
A Right **B** Wrong **C** Doesn't say

8 Asad is going to leave his home town in the future.
A Right **B** Wrong **C** Doesn't say

9 Asad wants to get a job working with computers.
A Right **B** Wrong **C** Doesn't say

I'm going to ... !

The future is so exciting! Why? Because we are going to do so many different things! Our magazine *Young People* looks at what some cool young people are going to do with their future.

Thirteen-year-old Wafi is from Cairo, Egypt. He says that he is going to be a famous football player one day. He is going to go to a sports school when he is sixteen to learn how to be the best football player in the world. He hopes he will get a lot of money for doing what he does best. He thinks he'll be a bit nervous when he plays in his first big competition, but he also thinks his team will win because they are going to practise hard and be ready.

Sylvia, fourteen, is from London, UK. She wants to be a famous actress in the future. She says that she is going to finish school and then she is going to go to drama school. While she is learning how to be a great actress, she is going to be in plays in the local theatre. She doesn't think she'll get married until she's thirty, but she says she'll probably have four or five children after she gets married.

Asad is thirteen and he is from Saudi Arabia. He told us that he can speak four languages and that he is going to travel around the world when he finishes school. He wants to travel for five or six years and then go to university to study computers. He thinks it will be hard to stop travelling, but that he has to go to university if he wants to get a good job in a big company. He believes he will be very successful some day.

2 Read the article again and write a word or short phrase to answer each question.

1 How old is Wafi?
____

2 What does Wafi do best?
____

3 What country is Sylvia from?
____

4 How many children will Sylvia have?
____

5 How many languages does Asad speak?
____

6 How many years will Asad travel for?
____

Wordpower!

3 **Choose the correct word.**

1 I don't know for **guess / sure**, but I think that man is a famous actor.
2 My son is a whizz **play / kid**; he's five and he can use a computer!
3 I don't know how old you are. Wait, let me **guess / program**.
4 My sister is going to go to drama **school / company** next year.
5 Dad, could you help me **program / guess** my laptop, please?
6 She's going to buy that successful computer **play / company**.
7 Look at this new phone **app / school**. Isn't it cool?
8 We are going to get tickets for the school **play / drama**. Do you want to come?

4 **Write a word from the box in each gap.**

apps • company • guess • kid • play • program • school • sure

Sheila Patterson is the most beautiful girl in my school. She's tall and slim and all the boys like her. I don't know for (1) __________, but I think she'll go to drama (2) __________ and be a famous actress some day. I'm going to see her in a(n) (3) __________ next week – it's at the local theatre here in our home town. I know she'll be amazing. Can you (4) __________ what I'm going to do in the future? I want to have my own computer (5) __________. I'm going to sell computers and make lots of money!
(Theresa Han, thirteen years old)

Theresa Han knows more than any other student in my school – she's a whizz (6) __________ and all the boys like her. She knows a lot about computers and she can (7) __________ them too. I think in the future she'll make (8) __________ for mobile phones and make thousands of euros! I'm so jealous of her!
(Sheila Patterson, thirteen years old)

Grammar 1

be going to

Look again at *Grammar database 21* on page 153 before doing these exercises.

1 **Complete the sentences with *be going to* and the verbs given.**

1 __________ (**you/go**) to university in the future?
2 She __________ (**not appear**) at the concert tonight.
3 __________ (**he/practise**) playing basketball after school today?
4 I __________ (**not see**) a play at the weekend.
5 Grant __________ (**be**) a pilot when he grows up.
6 Marta and Fazil __________ (**get**) ready for dinner in five minutes.
7 __________ (**I/develop**) a new app for mobile phones?
8 I __________ (**study**) English next year.
9 They __________ (**not work**) with computers when they are older.
10 Mum and I __________ (**visit**) the zoo in New York City.

2 Look at the picture. Write the correct form of *be going to* and a verb from the box in each gap.

brush • collect • feed • let • move • pick • plant • ride

1 Jane ______ the kitten.
2 Bach ______ the puppy.
3 Little Tom ______ the chickens go free!
4 Bob and Jake ______ vegetables.
5 The dog ______ the lambs to the big field.
6 Mum ______ the eggs.
7 Morris ______ the pony.
8 Suzy ______ a beautiful flower.

3 Look at the table and write questions and short answers using *be going to*.

	Work with computers	Be famous and successful
1 I	✔	✘
2 You	✘	✔
3 Ivan	✘	✔
4 Marta	✔	✘
5 Sven and Hans	✘	✔
6 Brendon and I	✘	✔

1 *Am I going to work with computers?* *Yes, I am.*
Am I going to be famous and successful? *No, I'm not.*

2 ______ ______
______ ______

3 ______ ______
______ ______

4 ______ ______
______ ______

5 ______ ______
______ ______

6 ______ ______
______ ______

Wordpower!

1 Write a phrase from the box in each gap.

a quarter of • a third of • all of • almost half of • almost all of • half of • ~~most of~~ • none of

1 80% *most of*
2 100% ____________
3 50% ____________
4 33% ____________
5 95% ____________
6 45% ____________
7 25% ____________
8 0% ____________

2 Choose the correct phrase.

1 **Half of / All of** the people we asked, or 100%, said they loved the new laptop.
2 **None of / Almost all of** the kids from my school will be at the concert – not even one.
3 We ate **most of / a third of** the pizza for lunch – there are only two pieces left.
4 **Almost half of / A quarter of** the people liked our new chocolate bar; that's only 25%!
5 **A third of / Almost all of** my friends think this book will be a bestseller – three out of nine of them.
6 **None of / Almost half of** the people in this room are going to be actors – that's about 45%.
7 **Almost all of / A quarter of** the people in this company work with computers – 95% in fact.
8 **Half of / A quarter of** the apps we develop are successful – the other 50% aren't very popular.

Listening

CD Track 14

1 Listen to two friends talking about what they and their friends are going to do in the future. Match the people (1–6) with what they are going to do (a–g). There is one letter you do not need to use.

1 Vera ___
2 Dimitris ___
3 Fazal ___
4 Julia ___
5 Kenny ___
6 Brad ___

a be a mechanic
b work for a games company
c program computers
d fly planes
e stay in his/her home town
f create apps
g go to drama school

CD Track 14

2 Listen to the conversation again and decide if these statements are true (T) or false (F).

1 Vera is a famous actress. T/F
2 Dimitris spends a lot of his time watching planes. T/F
3 Fazal enjoys working with cars. T/F
4 Julia spends a lot of time on the phone. T/F
5 Kenny is not going to play games often. T/F
6 Brad isn't going to do what his father does. T/F

Grammar 2

will

Look again at *Grammar database 22* on page 154 before doing these exercises.

1 Write P (for prediction), F (for facts) or I (asking for information).

1 London is expensive, so you'll need a lot of money. ___
2 Will Bob and Marta be at the play Friday night? ___
3 I think it'll rain later today. ___
4 These are on special offer, so they'll be cheap. ___
5 We believe my brother will be a successful farmer one day. ___
6 Will you be in New York in August? ___

2 Match.

1 I'm going to New York in December. I'm so excited! ___
2 Peter and Kenny never study. ___
3 Luke loves to read. ___
4 It's very hot in here. ___
5 Sam and I don't like flying. ___
6 Mum and Dad won two tickets to see *Scream 4*. ___
7 I'm going to a party tonight. ___
8 Dina is going to take drama lessons. ___

a She'll be a famous actress someday.
b They won't pass their exams.
c He'll like this book you got for him.
d We won't enjoy being on the plane.
e They won't like it; it's very scary.
f I know I'll love the sights.
g You're right. I'll open a window.
h On a Tuesday? Will you be in school tomorrow?

3 Write questions and answers using *will*.

1 What / weather / be like / Thursday? (rainy and cold)
Q: *What will the weather be like on Thursday?*
A: *I think it will be rainy and cold* .

2 What / time / you / go / Jane's party / Friday night? (eight o'clock)
Q: ______
A: I think ______ .

3 What / she / wear / to school / tomorrow? (skirt and T-shirt)
Q: ______
A: I think ______ .

4 What / I / see / on the farm / at the weekend? (lambs and chicks)
Q: ______
A: I think ______ .

5 What / job / Petros / have / when he's thirty? (pilot)
Q: ______
A: I think ______ .

6 What / they / do / on holiday? (nothing special)
Q: ______
A: I think ______ .

✓ Quick check

4 Choose the correct answer.

1 We use *be going to* to talk about future **plans / intentions / both.**
2 We use the same form of *be going to* for *I/you/he/we*. **yes / no**
3 Which one is correct? **They're go to travel to Kenya. / They're going to travel to Kenya. / both**
4 Which one is correct? **Sam's not going to go to university. / Sam isn't going to go to university. / both**
5 We use *will* to give information about future events and make predictions. **yes / no**
6 After *will/won't*, we use the bare infinitive. **yes / no**
7 We use the same form of *will/won't* for *I/you/he/we*. **yes / no**
8 Which one is correct? **He'll to be a successful adult. / He'll be a successful adult. / both**

Writing

1 Read the email and match each part of the email with a statement.

write reply send

1 ___ To: Alexis
2 ___ Subject: My plans for tomorrow
Hi, Alexis,
3 ___ I was sitting here thinking about the future and wanted to tell you what I'm going to do when I grow up. I'm going to work in a big games company.
4 ___ Isn't that exciting? I think they'll let me play games half of the day and I believe I'll get lots of money.
5 ___ Do you think about your future? What are you going to do when you finish school?
Take care!
Vito

a This part talks about predictions.
b This part asks the person reading the email to talk about their plans.
c This part shows who will read the email.
d This part talks about plans and intentions.
e This part says what the email is going to be about.

2 Read the email again and tick (✓) the statements that are correct.

The writer …

1 uses his friend's first name. ☐
2 says where he is writing the email. ☐
3 uses short forms. ☐
4 uses *be going to* for plans and intentions. ☐
5 uses *will* to make predictions about the future. ☐
6 writes his last name at the end of the email. ☐

12

Lights! Camera! Action!

Reading

1 Read the article and match each title with a paragraph.

a Give it all you've got
b Hobby for some, dream for others
c A special role
d One of the crowd
e You've seen them before

1 ___

An extra in a movie is an actor who doesn't speak. We see these actors in the background of a movie scene. Many movies have hundreds of extras. This is especially true for action movies that have got big scenes where many people are running from some dangerous event.

2 ___

But if an actor has just got one speaking part in a movie, they aren't an extra any more. What are they exactly then? They're not main actors, of course, you probably won't see their name at the start of the movie although sometimes they completely change the story in the movie. Their roles can be very important, even if they only say one single line. This kind of role is called a 'bit part'.

3 ___

A 'bit' is something really small. This is why we use this word to describe these very small parts. An actor who does these kinds of roles all the time is called a 'bit player'. Maybe you've seen an actor like this in more than one movie. You don't know who she or he is exactly but you think, hmm, where have I seen this actor before?

4 ___

There are a lot of actors who do bit parts as a hobby. They live near Hollywood and they've probably got other jobs. They also make good money doing bit parts. However, most actors do bit parts because they want bigger roles. This is true for most of today's famous actors.

5 ___

Sometimes, though, actors who do bit parts never get to do more than that. Still, it can be a really fun job. A famous acting teacher once said, 'There are no small parts, only small actors.' So if someone offers you a bit part, play the role like it's the role of a lifetime!

2 Read the article again and decide if the statements are true (T) or false (F).

1 Action movies often have hundreds of extras in them. T/F
2 If an actor says one line in a movie, their name is certain to appear at the start. T/F
3 A bit part always changes the story of a movie. T/F
4 Some actors only do bit parts. T/F
5 Most actors do bit parts for the money. T/F
6 If you want to be an important actor, you shouldn't take small roles. T/F

Wordpower!

3 **Choose the correct word or phrase.**

1 This cinema shows exciting new **roles / movies**.
2 I don't need much time to **prepare / shoot** for my part as an extra.
3 We got great seats in the cinema because it was **in the background / empty**.
4 His **scene / role** in the movie was as the best friend of the main character.
5 The director wants to **shoot / prepare** this part of the film in a restaurant.
6 It says there's a(n) **action movie / scene** on at the cinema at nine o'clock tonight.
7 I play an extra in the film, and I'll be standing **empty / in the background**.
8 I love the **scene / role** in the movie where the two main characters kiss.

4 **Write a word from the box in each gap.**

action • background • empty • movie • prepare • role • scene • shoot

Interviewer: Mr James, tell us about your new (1) __________ that's in cinemas later this year.

Rick James: Well, it's a(n) (2) __________ movie called *The Big Race*, and I play the (3) __________ of a racing car driver who loves racing and winning.

Interviewer: I see. What things did you do to (4) __________ for playing this character?

Rick James: I spent a lot of time with real racing car drivers. I learned what they do in real life. I also learned how to drive a racing car.

Interviewer: I see. Is there a particular (5) __________ in the film that's really exciting?

Rick James: There are many, actually. We were able to (6) __________ the film at a real racing event with real racing car drivers. You will see most of them in the (7) __________. They will definitely make the film seem real.

Interviewer: That sounds very exciting. I'm sure there won't be any (8) __________ seats in the cinema.

Rick James: I hope not!

Grammar 1 G

Present continuous for future arrangements

Look again at *Grammar database 23* on page 154 before doing these exercises.

1 **Write the verbs in the present continuous.**

1 She __________ (**prepare**) for tomorrow's scene tonight.
2 They __________ (**do**) my make-up at two this afternoon.
3 I __________ (**get**) paid for the part this evening.
4 We __________ (**shoot**) the scene later today.
5 He __________ (**take**) Marty to the studio at nine.
6 You __________ (**not give**) an interview to the magazine today.

2 Write a verb from the box in each gap in the present continuous.

go • have • not meet • not try on • play • shoot

1 I __________ to the studio this morning.
2 We __________ the director later today.
3 She __________ the role of a singer in her next film.
4 They __________ lunch at a Chinese restaurant at 1.
5 We __________ the last scene this afternoon.
6 I __________ the costumes tomorrow.

3 Look at the information and complete the gaps.

7am	– arrive at the studio		1pm	– have lunch
7.30am	– have a meeting with the director		2pm	– change costumes, play role as extra
8am	– visit the make-up area		2.45pm	– start the second scene (no preparing)
8.45am	– put on costume		4.30pm	– finish the scene
9.30am	– prepare for the first scene		5pm	– leave the studio and go home
10.30am	– shoot the first scene			

Maggie: Let's talk about what you're doing tomorrow, George.

George: Yes, thank you. I know that I (1) __________ at the studio at 7 and we (2) __________ the first scene at 10.30. Oh, and we (3) __________ for the day at 5.

Maggie: Yes, that's correct. So, you (4) __________ the make-up area at 8. Then you (5) __________ your costume at 8.45. At 9.30 you (6) __________ for the first scene.

George: How long do you think the first scene will take?

Maggie: Probably two hours, maybe a little longer. We (7) __________ lunch at 1 so we should finish the first scene before then. Then, you'll have an hour for lunch at the studio, and you (8) __________ costumes for the second scene at 2.

George: Is there going to be time to prepare for the second scene?

Maggie: No, you (9) __________ for the second scene at all. You (10) __________ the role of an extra so you don't need to prepare. It'll be easy, don't worry. We (11) __________ the second scene at 2.45, and we (12) __________ it at 4.30. And that's about it!

George: OK, great. Thanks for letting me know.

Maggie: You're welcome!

Wordpower!

1 Write a word in each gap to complete the sentences. The first letter is given to help you.

1 This place is so high, it nearly touches the sky. **m** ___ ___ ___ ___ ___ ___ ___
2 If you jump from this, you could die. **c** ___ ___ ___ ___
3 This place hasn't got any water. **d** ___ ___ ___ ___ ___
4 You can walk or drive over this and see farm animals. **f** ___ ___ ___ ___
5 This is a place where you can have fun right by the sea. **b** ___ ___ ___ ___
6 There are many trees, birds and wild animals in this place. **f** ___ ___ ___ ___ ___
7 This is full of water and you can travel over it in a boat. **l** ___ ___ ___

2 Read these statements and decide where these people are, using words from Exercise 1.

1 'We're having a great time here, aren't we? The sun is warm, the sand is nice and the water looks beautiful.'
They're at the ___________.
2 'Stop! You must be very careful. If you fall, you'll get hurt or even die.' They're on a ___________.
3 'It's very cold here and there's snow from here all the way to the top, but the view is amazing!'
He's on a ___________.
4 'There's a lot of wind today, so we can sail around very easily.'
They're on a ___________.
5 'Wow, it's beautiful here. And look at the horses running through the grass! How nice!'
They're in a ___________.
6 'It's very difficult to walk here. It's very hot and dry, there's no water and I can't see because there's sand in my eyes.'
She's in a ___________.
7 'Oh, no! I think I saw a bear. Look – it's hiding behind the trees. I think we should leave now.'
They're in a ___________.

Listening

CD Track 15

1 Listen to two people talking about a movie and match the scenes with the places. There are two letters you do not need to use.

1 Scene 1 ___
2 Scene 2 ___
3 Scene 3 ___
4 Scene 4 ___
5 Scene 5 ___
6 Scene 6 ___

a open fields
b the beach
c a train
d a forest
e a lake
f a cliff
g the mountains
h the city

CD Track 15

2 Listen to the conversation again and for each question, choose the correct answer, A, B or C.

1 Who does James Z fight at Dr Wam's house?
A a bad guy **B** Dr Wam **C** a group of guys
2 Who is in front of James Z when he jumps from the cliff?
A Dr Wam **B** no-one **C** the bad guys
3 Where does James Z land after he jumps from the cliff?
A on a train **B** in a forest **C** in a lake
4 Where does James Z fight the bad guys in the fifth scene?
A inside the train **B** on top of the train **C** inside a train station
5 How does James Z get off the train?
A He falls. **B** He jumps. **C** He runs.
6 What does Lady Q do in the end of the movie?
A She fights the bad guys. **B** She fights James Z. **C** She helps Dr Wam.

Grammar 2

G

Prepositions of time and place

Look again at *Grammar database 24* on page 154 before doing these exercises.

1 Match.

1 We're meeting this evening at ___
2 I'm going by ___
3 We're shooting today in front of ___
4 They're filming the second scene in ___
5 The extras are standing next ___
6 The first day of shooting is on ___
7 The main character is walking out ___
8 They're going ___

a the post office.
b home later today.
c to the police car.
d Monday.
e eight o'clock.
f the afternoon.
g of the kitchen.
h plane if it's not too expensive.

2 Write a word from the box in each gap.

at • by • for • into • near • on

1 Paul's an actor and he lives ___________ London.
2 We're filming the last scene ___________ 3rd March.
3 Helen's not here right now. She's ___________ work.
4 Jill opened her front door and walked ___________ her house.
5 We flew to the movie studio ___________ helicopter. Can you believe it?
6 We waited for the director ___________ two hours.

3 Read the text and for each question, choose the correct answer, A, B or C.

	A	B	C
1	**A** in	**B** to	**C** on
2	**A** at	**B** on	**C** next
3	**A** to	**B** in	**C** at
4	**A** on	**B** at	**C** in
5	**A** by	**B** on	**C** at
6	**A** near	**B** on	**C** in
7	**A** in	**B** at	**C** by
8	**A** in	**B** to	**C** on
9	**A** at	**B** to	**C** into
10	**A** on	**B** in	**C** at
11	**A** on	**B** to	**C** in
12	**A** to	**B** by	**C** on
13	**A** in	**B** for	**C** to
14	**A** in	**B** at	**C** on
15	**A** on	**B** in	**C** at

http://www.tonyblog.co.uk

Home | Archive | Links | Contact me

TONY'S BLOG

SATURDAY NIGHT MOVIE

I really enjoy James Bond films. My friend Louis and I are planning to watch *Casino Royale* (1) ___ TV (2) ___ Louis's house (3) ___ the weekend. I'm excited because it's my favourite James Bond film. I first saw it (4) ___ 2006 (5) ___ the cinema (6) ___ my house. One of my favourite parts (7) ___ the movie is when James Bond goes (8) ___ a journey (9) ___ an island (10) ___ the Caribbean Sea to look for information about a man. There are some scenes (11) ___ the beach that are really great. Then he goes (12) ___ plane (13) ___ America to stop a scary event from happening. Later he's (14) ___ Europe playing cards with some dangerous characters. It's very exciting! Well, the movie's starting (15) ___ 9pm. It's going to be great!

Quick check

4 Choose the correct answer.

1 Can we use the present continuous to describe future arrangements? **yes / no**
2 Can we use the present simple to describe future arrangements? **yes / no**
3 Which is correct? **What are you doing tonight? / What do you do tonight? / both**
4 Do we use *at* before times, *on* before days and *in* before months? **yes / no**
5 Can we use *near, next to, in front of* and *in* before places? **yes / no**
6 The correct answer to *Where are you?* is: **I'm at the home. / I'm at home. / both**

Writing

1 Read the interview and match each question (a–f) with a gap in the interview.

Working in Film

This week's interview is with 28-year-old Matt Warren. He talks to us about what he does in movies and why he got started doing it.

So, Matt, you work in films. (1) _d_
Sure, Dale. I work as a writer for the movies. Actually, I'm called a 'screenwriter'.
That's interesting. (2) ___
Of course. A screenwriter is someone who writes the story of a movie. We write the words that the actors say. We also write the action of the movie, such as what actors do in different scenes. Why they move, where the action happens, and so on.
In other words, you write the movie. (3) ___
For about five years. I started when I was 23. I was writing film reviews for a local newspaper when I got the idea to become a screenwriter.
It sounds like you really like films. (4) ___
Well, there is one movie in the cinema now, *Russian Holiday*, about a family that travels to Russia and gets into some serious trouble. It's an action movie.
That sounds exciting. (5) ___
Yes. I'm working on another action movie. I'm finishing it in about a month.
That's great. (6) ___
In about nine months. At least I hope so.

a Can we see your work in any recent movies?
b How long have you had this job?
c When is the movie coming to cinemas?
d Can you tell us what you do?
e Are you working on anything right now?
f Can you tell us what that is?

2 Read the interview again and write a word or phrase to complete the sentences.

1 Matt's job in film is to write the __________ of a movie.
2 One part of his job is to write what the actors __________.
3 Matt also writes what actors do in different __________.
4 Before he started working as a screenwriter, Matt wrote __________.
5 *Russian Holiday*, is a(n) __________.
6 His next movie is in cinemas in about __________.

Check your progress! | Units 11-12

1 Read the text and for each question, choose the correct answer A, B or C.

It may seem like an easy job, but acting in the (1) ___ is harder than it looks. If you're interested in acting, the first step is to take classes at a(n) (2) ___. (3) ___ today's famous actors studied acting before they got their important (4) ___. It's important to study acting so you know how to (5) ___ for a part. You also learn things like where to stand when the director is (6) ___ the film. Acting lessons can also help young actors to know (7) ___ if this is what they really want to do. Many young actors start by acting in (8) ___ before they go on to shooting a film. When actors start doing movies, (9) ___ them play small parts in the (10) ___ as extras. Then, if they're lucky, they get bigger parts and one day, they become stars!

	A	B	C
1	**A** roles	**B** scenes	**C** movies
2	**A** company	**B** app	**C** drama school
3	**A** A quarter	**B** Almost all of	**C** None of
4	**A** scenes	**B** plays	**C** roles
5	**A** programme	**B** guess	**C** prepare
6	**A** preparing	**B** shooting	**C** programming
7	**A** for sure	**B** sure	**C** certain
8	**A** forests	**B** beaches	**C** plays
9	**A** almost all	**B** most of	**C** almost half
10	**A** role	**B** action movie	**C** background

10 marks

2 Write sentences and questions using the correct form of *be going to*.

11 I / wear / my jacket / tomorrow.

____

12 you / travel / to Spain / next week?

____

13 Rachel / practise / music / tonight.

____

14 we / study / for the maths test / later?

____

15 Ben and Steve / play / football / this weekend.

____

5 marks

3 Write sentences and questions using *will*.

16 the classes / be / difficult?

____

17 Jake / enjoy / the gift / very much.

____

18 I / not go / to university / in the summer.

____

19 it / be / hot / in Greece?

____

20 we / do / well / on our exams.

____

5 marks

4 Choose the correct word or phrase.

21 **Are / Will** we meeting Tim at 10am today?
22 I'm **play / playing** the part of a teacher in this film.
23 They **are not / won't** practising the scene after lunch.
24 The movie is showing **in 9pm at Wednesday / at 9pm on Wednesday**.
25 I'm **at home on 4th April / on home next 4th April**.

5 marks

Total:____ / 25 marks

13

Raising Money!

Reading

1 Read the text about raising money for a charity and for each question, choose the correct answer, A, B or C.

1 Katherine Burn's text is …

A a short story.
B an article.
C an email.

2 Katherine …

A goes to Greenfields Primary School.
B doesn't have enough food to eat.
C thinks the world is a fair place.

3 Market Day …

A is on a weekday.
B will be in a supermarket.
C will raise money.

4 Katherine says they have got …

A twenty new CDs to sell.
B cakes from a local shop.
C twenty books from a bookshop.

DOING YOUR BIT FOR CHARITY

by Katherine Burns

The world is a strange place, and it isn't always a fair place – some people are rich and some people are poor. In some parts of the world, children don't have enough food to eat or enough money to buy clothes or shoes. Every year at Greenfields Primary School, we do something to raise money for these children. This year we've decided to have a Market Day.

On Market Day, on Saturday 4th December, we are going to make our school look just like a big shopping centre! People can come any time from 9am to 5pm and buy everything from clothes to CDs, cakes and flowers! My team and I have been very busy. There has been a lot to do to prepare for this big charity event, but there is more to do, and we need your help.

Bill Thomas has visited local shops and asked them to give us things that we can sell at the event. Bookworm Bookshop has sent us twenty new books and Mel's Music Shop has offered to give us thirty new CDs. We haven't gone to get those, so we need someone to do that.

Philip Polanski and Khan Duong have emailed all the teachers and asked them to come to our event, and Ned Campbell has put a message on the school website saying the event is open to the public.

Last year, Ms Grant and Ms Ali made some wonderful cakes for our charity event. Luckily for us, they have said they will do it again this year. They have bought the flour and all the other ingredients and they are going to make the cakes, over fifty, on the Friday before Market Day. We want students to give us things that we can sell – old toys, games, clothes, anything that we can sell to make money for poor children.

Please do your bit for charity on Market Day!

2 Read the text again and tick (✓) the things people have done to prepare for the event.

1 People have decided what kind of event to have. ___
2 The students have made the school look like a shopping centre. ___
3 Someone has asked local shops to give things for Market Day. ___
4 Someone has gone to Mel's Music Shop to get the CDs. ___
5 Philip and Khan have sent emails. ___
6 Ned has put a message on the school website. ___
7 Someone has bought the things to make the cakes. ___
8 Ms Grant and Ms Ali have made fifty cakes. ___

Wordpower!

3 Each of the words in bold is in the wrong sentence. Write a word in bold from another sentence to replace the incorrect one.

1 I've decided to **raise** the Boston Marathon this year! ________
2 Tony isn't **local**! He's got a huge house and an expensive car. ________
3 My class wants to **enter** money for the poor children in Somalia. ________
4 My uncle is a **poor** actor and he gives a lot of money to children in Africa. ________
5 My parents give money to the **messy** *WWF* every year. ________
6 Look at this room! Why are you so **rich**, Judy? ________
7 Have you seen that the **marathon** butcher's on the high street has closed? ________
8 Has your dad ever run a **charity**? ________

4 Write a word from the box in each gap.

charity • enter • local • messy • poor • raise • rich

Some people in the world are (1) ________ and have lots to eat, and some are (2) ________ and don't have shoes to wear on their feet. It's not fair, but that's the way it is. Have you got time to help people that aren't as lucky as you are? Why don't you (3) ________ this year's *Baked Beans Bath* event? This event is a part of the bigger event, *Food for Africa*, to (4) ________ money for hungry children. Come to the (5) ________ school on Elm Road to do your part – sitting in baked beans will be (6) ________, but it will help a very important (7) ________.

Grammar 1 G

Present perfect simple (*ever, never*)

Look again at *Grammar database 25* on page 154 before doing these exercises.

1 Each of the words or phrases in bold is incorrect. Write the correct words on the lines.

1 Has he ever **give** money to charity? ________
2 Has she **never see** that action movie? ________
3 Don't worry. The pilot has **fly** a plane before. ________
4 I **has be** to this restaurant before. ________
5 **Has we raise** enough money for the local school? ________
6 I've **ever visit** the UK. Is it nice there? ________
7 Good, **you's** bought all the ingredients for the cake. ________
8 Sheila hasn't **never** run in a marathon. ________

2 Look at the information and answer the questions.

you	–	put a message on the website
Sheila	–	make lots of cakes
Tom	–	sell fifty tickets
Ali and Sam	–	go to the local shops
Bookworm Bookshop	–	give us twenty new books
You and Matt	–	bring old clothes to sell

1 What have you done? *I have put a message on the website.*
2 What has Sheila done? ____________
3 What has Tom done? ____________
4 What have Ali and Sam done? ____________
5 What has the Bookworm Bookshop done? ____________
6 What have you and Matt done? ____________

3 Use the answers in Exercise 2 to write negative statements.

1 *I haven't put a message on the website.*
2 ____________
3 ____________
4 ____________
5 ____________
6 ____________

4 Write the verbs in the present perfect simple.

I (1) ____________ (**work**) a lot, and I (2) ____________ (**save**) a lot of money. I (3) ____________ (**be**) very lucky and successful, so I (4) ____________ (**give**) a lot of money to charity. My wife and I raise money for *Feed the Children* every year. It is a charity that (5) ____________ (**do**) a lot for poor children all around the world. (6) ____________ (**you ever help**) a charity? Next week, there is a marathon in my city. The city (7) ____________ (**not have**) a marathon before, so everyone is very excited. I (8) ____________ (**enter**) and I (9) ____________ (**ask**) all my friends to enter, too. (10) ____________ (**anyone tell**) you about this event? You can read about it on the website runforcharity.com. Someone (11) ____________ (**put**) a message about it on there. If you (12) ____________ (**not do**) your bit for charity, now is the time!

Wordpower!

1 Look at the picture and decide if the statements are true (T) or false (F).

1 Below the MARKET DAY sign, someone is selling books and CDs. T/F
2 On top of the CDs are some books. T/F
3 Between the books are some CDs. T/F
4 Underneath the table with hats and shoes on it are some old clothes. T/F
5 Beside the stall selling hats and shoes there is a stall selling hot dogs. T/F
6 Behind the table with hot dogs on it is a person dressed as a big dog. T/F
7 Over the table with hot dogs on it there is lots of mustard. T/F
8 Above the hot dog stall is a sign saying how much the hot dogs cost. T/F

2 Rewrite the words to complete the gaps in the text.

I'm at a fair in the local school. The students decided to have the fair to raise money for charity. See that sign – the one (1) ____________ (**vreo**) the door? It says that the fair is for the charity *WWF*. Look over there. That's my friend (2) ____________ (**dnihbe**) the table at the stall selling cakes. See all the cakes on (3) ____________ (**pto**) of the table? My Mum made those – she loves doing things for charity. There's the hot dog stall. Look, the sign (4) ____________ (**evbao**) it says the hot dogs cost one euro; that's not expensive. Oh, look. There is a dog (5) ____________ (**thnaerednu**) the table, and he looks hungry! That's my sister, Suzie, at the stall selling old books and CDs. And that's her best friend (6) ____________ (**ebedis**) her. See them? There – at the stall (7) ____________ (**eenwebt**) the hot dog stall and the cakes stall. You still can't see them? There! (8) ____________ (**woleb**) the sign that says 'GOOD AS NEW'.

Listening

CD Track 16

1 Listen to three people talking about charity events and for each question, choose the correct answer, A, B or C.

1 The telethon raises money to buy food for the poor.
A Right **B** Wrong **C** Doesn't say

2 Enid knows some of the people she has spoken to.
A Right **B** Wrong **C** Doesn't say

3 To raise money, Asad is cleaning cars.
A Right **B** Wrong **C** Doesn't say

4 Asad's local pool is closed at weekends.
A Right **B** Wrong **C** Doesn't say

5 Angela learned about the children in Africa online.
A Right **B** Wrong **C** Doesn't say

6 Angela walks people's dogs when they are at work.
A Right **B** Wrong **C** Doesn't say

CD Track 17

2 **Listen to the first speaker again and complete the gaps.**

Name of event: (1) ____________ the World Telethon

When: (2) ____________ December

Time: 9am to (3) ____________ pm

Name of speaker: Enid Smith

Number of people Enid has spoken to in the morning: more than (4) ____________

Money Enid raised in the morning: about (5) ____________

Grammar 2

G

Adverbs of manner

Look again at *Grammar database 26* on page 155 before doing these exercises.

1 **Choose the correct word.**

1 Mum put the books on the glass table **carefully / careful**.
2 Kevin finished the marathon **sucessfuly / succesfully**.
3 Sue has a problem with her leg; she can't walk very **quickly / quick**.
4 Why are you talking so **loudly / loud**? I'm here beside you!
5 Dad used the sharp knife **nervousily / nervously**.
6 I didn't know Ivan wrote so **good / well**. I loved his short story!
7 Timothy won the swimming race **easyly / easily**.
8 Raising money is **hardly / hard**, but we have to help the poor children.
9 My parents were happy I got home **safely / safly**.
10 Look at Pete go! He can run very **fastly / fast**.

2 **Put a line through the incorrect sentence.**

1 Why are you eating so fast? / Why are you so fastly eating?
2 Tanya whispered quietly to her best friend. / Tanya quiet whispered to her best friend.
3 My mum makes cakes very good. / My mum makes cakes very well.
4 Our team won easily the match. / Our team won the match easily.
5 The little girl stroked the lamb gently. / The little girl stroked the lamb gentle.
6 Grandma sang happily in the garden. / Grandma happy sang in the garden.
7 Gerrard tried hard, but wasn't successful. / Gerrard hardly tried, but he wasn't successful.
8 Bob plays the piano very badly. / Bob plays the piano very bad.

Quick check

3 **Choose the correct answer.**

1 The exact time is important when we use present perfect simple. **yes / no**
2 We can use *ever* in questions using the present perfect simple. **yes / no**
3 We use the past participle to form the present perfect simple. **yes / no**
4 Which one is correct? **Have you ever run in a marathon? / Have you ever ran in a marathon? / both**
5 We use adverbs of manner to describe how someone does something. **yes / no**
6 Which one is correct? **My sister cooks very good. / My sister cooks very well. / both**

Writing

1 **Read the text and for each question, choose the correct answer, A, B or C.**

1 What kind of text is it?
A an email
B an article
C a blog

2 What did Sam do to raise money for charity on Saturday?
A ate hot dogs
B sold things
C had a concert

3 How much money did Sam raise?
A fifty euro
B eight euro
C five euro

2 **Read the text again and underline all the adverbs of manner.**

http://www.samblog.co.uk

Home | Archive | Links | Contact me

Sam has his say!

December 14th

Doing my bit for charity!

Hi, everyone, welcome back. Today, I'm going to tell you about what my school did to raise money for the charity *WWF* on Saturday.

My school has raised money for charity successfully lots of times. One year, we had a concert and the money from the tickets helped build a school in Africa. Another time, we had a Market Day where we sold things to raise money. This year, the school decided to do something we've never done before – we had a hot-dog-eating marathon!

Students had to eat lots and lots of hot dogs, and they had to eat them fast! I had a plan, I ate the hot dogs slowly at first, but then, after two or three, I ate really fast. Some of the students did well, but I won the marathon easily. I ate eight hot dogs in five minutes and raised over fifty euros for charity! I didn't do badly, did I? Have you ever raised money for charity? Leave a comment below.

14

Looking Ahead!

Reading

1 Read the article and write 'K' for Kyle, 'D' for Debbie or 'S' for Shawna.

www.science4ourkids.co.uk

Home | News in Science | Articles | Important Links

CAN YOU SEE THE FUTURE?

We asked some students to tell us what they think life will be like in a decade. Here are their predictions.

Kyle, 13
Cardiff, UK
Well, in ten years I'll be twenty-three years old. I'll probably finish university before then. I hope life will be great, but it's hard to say. If scientists and doctors discover better ways to help sick people, then maybe our world won't have sick people in it any more. Or at least not people who are really sick. That would be a great world to live in. I might even become a doctor or a scientist at university. If I do that, I will try to help people a lot.

Debbie, 12
Glasgow, UK
Ten years is a really long time! I hope we will travel in space more. That seems like an exciting thing to do. If technology improves, I think we will find a way to get to the moon more easily. I also think we'll even go past the moon some day. If we find a way to travel really fast, we will travel all the way to Mars. I think it will be probably a scary journey. But if scientists build a strong ship for space travel, the journey will be safe. And I want to go!

Shawna, 14
Sydney, Australia
I really hope life will be easier for all of us in ten years. These days, it seems like we work too much. If we find a way to work less but get more done then life will be much better than it is now. I think technology has a role in making that happen. We need to build better machines. If we build better machines that do the same things people do but much faster, we will all work less! Who wouldn't like that?

In ten years, this person hopes …

1 we will all work a lot less. ___
2 people will be healthier. ___
3 we can travel far away. ___
4 machines will improve. ___
5 to travel to another planet. ___
6 to finish studying completely. ___

2 Read the article again and write one or two words in each gap.

1 Kyle will be ____________ in ten years.
2 Kyle would like to work as a doctor or a ____________ some day.
3 Debbie thinks people will find a way to get to the ____________ more easily.
4 Debbie thinks the ____________ to Mars would be scary.
5 Shawna thinks technology has a ____________ in helping us work less.
6 Shawna thinks machines might be able to work ____________ than people.

Wordpower!

3 Each of the words in bold is in the wrong sentence. Write a word in bold from another sentence to replace the incorrect one.

1 I can't drive because I didn't bring my **predictions**. ______
2 Where will you go to **technology** after you finish school? ______
3 There are millions of stars in the **licence**. ______
4 Every year we see faster and better computers, thanks to **scientist**. ______
5 What are your **university** for next year's most popular jobs? ______
6 Did you **move** a job with the computer maker? ______
7 I want to be a **universe** someday and study the stars. ______
8 Are you going to **apply for** to a new town when you're older? ______

4 Write a word or phrase from the box in each gap.

apply for • licence • move • prediction • scientist • universe • university

Frank: Will you go to (1) ______ someday, Trish?

Trish: I believe so, Frank. I want to be a (2) ______ when I'm older and study plants. Actually, I'd like to (3) ______ to the countryside someday so I can be closer to them.

Frank: Ah, I really like the countryside. If I get my (4) ______ this year, we can drive there and look at the different plants and trees.

Trish: That's a great idea! We can go to New Forest Park. I'm going to (5) ______ a summer job there.

Frank: My dad and I went there for the weekend once. There are many green areas and you can see all the stars in the (6) ______ at night!

Trish: Cool! Well, I hope I get the job.

Frank: My (7) ______ is that you will. You really seem to love plants. You're perfect for the job!

Trish: Thanks. I'll let you know if I get it.

Grammar 1 G

First conditional

Look again at *Grammar database 27* on page155 before doing these exercises.

1 Tick (✔) the correct sentences. Underline the mistake in the incorrect sentences and write the correct word.

1 If I'll get a good job, they'll pay me lots of money. ___ ______
2 If I go to university, I don't become a teacher. ___ ______
3 If you'll study a lot for this test, the teacher will give you a good mark. ___ ______
4 If you don't make new friends at this school, you hate it. ___ ______
5 If you'll travel with me this summer, we'll have lots of fun. ___ ______
6 If I drive you to the airport, you'll get there faster. ___ ______
7 I won't see them every day if they'll move to a new town. ___ ______
8 If they visit London, Bobby and his uncle will go to the London Eye. ___ ______

2 Choose the correct word or phrase.

1 If Rachel goes to Paris, she **will meet / meets** interesting people.
2 **I'll / I** invite Mark to the party if you say it's OK.
3 I **won't / don't** go to work tomorrow if the weather's bad.
4 If you visit me this weekend, **we'll / we** play cards.
5 His life **will change / changes** if he decides to leave home.
6 If **I / I'll** get a kitten for my birthday, I'll call it Sammy.

3 Write sentences using the first conditional.

1 If / I / get / the job / I / buy / dinner
If I get the job, I'll buy dinner.
2 We / call / you / if / we / get lost
____
3 If / they / meet / they / like / each other
____
4 I / give / you / this phone / if / I / get / a new
____
5 If / you / see / this movie / you / love / it
____
6 Life / be / easier / if / technology / improve
____

4 Read the text and for each question, choose the correct answer, A, B or C.

write reply send

To: george16@mail.com

From: lesliem@fastmail.com

Subject: mountain trip

Hi, George,

How are you? I wanted to ask you about the trip to the mountains this weekend. Are we staying with Jackie? If we stay with her, it (1) ___ a lot of fun. And how are we getting there? If we (2) ___, we'll get there quicker. I don't know if you can take your parents' car. I think if we (3) ___ the bus, it will be easier, and it's not expensive. If we take an extra 20 euros with us, that (4) ___ for the bus tickets. When are we leaving on Saturday? If we (5) ___ in the morning, we'll have more time to spend in the mountains, of course. But maybe you can't leave early. I know you have to work at the bike shop that morning. If you (6) ___, maybe the shop owner will give you the day off. I was also thinking about activities to do while we're there. If the weather (7) ___ nice, we'll do lots of things outside, like go for a walk in the forest. But if it's rainy, we (8) ___ inside and play cards. What do you think?

Bye for now,

Leslie

	A	B	C
1	**A** is	**B** be	**C** will be
2	**A** drive	**B** will drive	**C** are driving
3	**A** will	**B** will take	**C** take
4	**A** pay	**B** paid	**C** will pay
5	**A** are leaving	**B** leave	**C** will leave
6	**A** will ask	**B** ask	**C** are asking
7	**A** is being	**B** is	**C** will be
8	**A** stayed	**B** stay	**C** will stay

Wordpower!

1 Choose the correct word.

1 This isn't the right way. We have to **go / turn** around.
2 When you get to King Street, **go / cross** straight on and my house is the fourth house on the right.
3 **Turn / Go** left at the museum and go to my office at 54 Nichols Street.
4 After you **cross / go** past the library, you'll see my house on the left.
5 I don't think we can go down this street. We'll have to **turn / cross** back.
6 To get to the theatre, **cross / go** the road and you'll see it on the right.
7 When you get to the traffic lights, **cross / turn** right and drive another two blocks.
8 When you see the police station, **turn / go** straight ahead and you'll see me standing on the right.

2 Read the text and for each question, choose the correct answer, A, B or C.

Margie: So, we're on Long Street. When we get to the library, (1) ___ left onto North Street.
Erica: Ah, I see it. OK.
Margie: Then, we (2) ___ past the supermarket and at the crossroads, we turn (3) ___ onto Elm street.
Erica: OK. There's the supermarket, and I'm turning now.
Margie: There's a police station at the end of the block. Don't turn left or right here – (4) ___ the road and keep going – Jill's house is the third house on the left.
Erica: OK. Hmm, I don't see the police station. Maybe we need to (5) ___ around.
Margie: Let me give Jill a call … Hi Jill, it's Margie.
Jill: Hi, Margie. Where are you?
Margie: We're on Elm Street. I think we're lost.
Jill: You are! When you get to the crossroads, go (6) ___ on. Pine Street is the next street.
Margie: Oh, yes, I read the directions wrong.
Jill: So, you should turn (7) ___ now and get back on North Street. On North Street, go straight (8) ___ and you'll see Pine Street.

1 **A** cross **B** go **C** turn
2 **A** turn **B** go **C** cross
3 **A** round **B** back **C** right
4 **A** cross **B** turn **C** back
5 **A** straight **B** turn **C** go
6 **A** ahead **B** back **C** straight
7 **A** back **B** on **C** ahead
8 **A** past **B** ahead **C** back

Listening

CD Track 18

1 Listen to two teenagers talking and put the directions from Martin's house to his new school in order.

1 ___ **a** Turn left onto Market Street.
2 ___ **b** Turn right onto Crabtree Road.
3 ___ **c** Go straight down East Road.
4 ___ **d** Go to the crossroads on Crabtree Road.
5 ___ **e** Go past the clothes shop.

CD Track 18

2 Listen to the conversation again and choose the correct answer.

1 Martin's house is on **East Road / Market Street**.
2 Angie's favourite clothes shop is on **Market Street / Crabtree Road**.
3 Martin has to travel for **10 minutes / 20 minutes** on Market Street.
4 Martin says you turn right onto Crabtree Road at the **crossroads / police station**.
5 When Martin's dad made a wrong turn on Crabtree Road, they **turned back / went straight on**.

Grammar 2

G

Adverbs of degree

Look again at *Grammar database 28* on page 155 before doing these exercises.

1 For each question, choose the correct phrase, A or B.

1 It's ___ to study hard.
A important quite **B** quite important
2 Mark doesn't enjoy ___.
A very much school **B** school very much
3 I'm ___ of money!
A nearly out **B** out nearly
4 Do you have ___?
A a lot to work **B** to work a lot
5 This is an ___ computer.
A extremely old **B** old extremely
6 Wendy walked ___ to arrive in time.
A really quickly **B** quickly really
7 Are we ___ yet?
A there almost **B** almost there
8 It was ___ of you to come to the party.
A very nice **B** nice very

2 Put the words into the correct order to make sentences.

1 nice / She's / doctor. / really / a
____
2 a / upset / You / lot. / me
____
3 at / good / quite / They're / maths.
____
4 an / desert / is / place. / hot / extremely / The
____
5 very / don't / science / I / much. / like
____
6 bags. / lost / She / her / almost
____
7 his / very / He's / job. / good / at
____
8 homework. / nearly / to / I / do / my / forgot
____

3 Write a word from the box in each gap.

extremely • lot • much • nearly • quite • really

Sarah: What kind of job do you want to do?
John: I think I want to be a doctor. It's a(n) (1) ___________ important job, and I'm interested in studying it very (2) ___________.
Sarah: That's good. Doesn't it take (3) ___________ a long time to become a doctor? Are you sure that's what you want to do?
John: Well, it's my last year in high school and I'm (4) ___________ finished, so I'll start university soon. I've thought about it a (5) ___________, and I've decided that it's a(n) (6) ___________ amazing job.
Sarah: Yes, it seems like you know what you want. Good luck with that!
John: Thanks!

Quick check

4 Choose the correct answer.

1 Do we use the *if* clause of the first conditional to talk about the result of a situation? **yes / no**
2 Do we use *will* in the other clause of the first conditional to talk about possible situations in the future? **yes / no**
3 Which is correct? **I'll go, if you go. / If you go, I'll go. / both**
4 Do we use adverbs of degree to describe how small something is? **yes / no**
5 Do we use adverbs of degree to show how much there is of something? **yes / no**
6 Which is correct? **She's quite a good friend. / She's a really good friend. / both**

Writing

1 Read the article and for each question, choose the correct answer, A or B.

Why I want to be a scientist

I don't know if being a scientist is a popular job, but I really want to be one. If I become a scientist, I will discover so many things. I just know it!
And of course, if I discover many things, I will make a lot of money. If I make a lot of money, I will give some of the money back to science. Then other scientists can discover more things. And I think discovering new things helps people, and that makes me very happy.

There's another thing I can do with the money I make from science. I might build smart places for scientists to work. If these places have amazing machines, scientists will probably find it easier to do their work. Maybe other scientists will do the same thing as me. They might give money back to science also. Then science will become the best it can be.

I know when I get older I may want to do something else in life. I'm quite young at the moment, but I'm really interested in science. I will continue to study it, and perhaps I'll be the next Albert Einstein some day!

1 The writer thinks if he becomes a scientist, …
A it will become a job everyone likes. **B** he will find things for the first time.
2 If the writer makes a lot of money, he will …
A give it to people. **B** use it to make science better.
3 The writer says it will make him happy if …
A science helps people. **B** people learn about science.
4 The writer wants to use the money he makes from science to build …
A new machines. **B** new work places.
5 The writer hopes other scientists will …
A do what he will do. **B** give money to him.
6 The writer is certain that he …
A will become a scientist. **B** enjoys studying science.

2 Rewrite the sentences using the words in bold.

1 I will be rich someday. **probably** ______________________
2 When I get older, I will change jobs. **might** ______________________
3 I'll be a famous singer. **maybe** ______________________
4 I will give some money to poor people. **may** ______________________
5 I'll build nice places to work. **perhaps** ______________________

Check your progress! | Units 13-14

1 For each question, choose the correct answer, A or B.

1 I will be upset if I don't get my driving ___ when I'm eighteen.
A university **B** licence
2 People make a lot of ___ , but no-one knows for sure what the future will be like.
A predictions **B** charities
3 Go ___ on and you'll come to a crossroads.
A straight **B** above
4 We don't really want to ___ house, but my dad got a job in New York.
A enter **B** move
5 We should ___ some money for those children – they need our help.
A cross **B** raise
6 If Santos ___ for the job, he will get it.
A applies **B** enters
7 Why are your shoes ___ the kitchen table?
A on top of **B** between
8 You're going the wrong way – you'll have to turn ___.
A over **B** around

8 marks

2 Choose the correct word or phrase.

9 Why is she screaming so **loud / loudly**?
10 The book was **quite / extremely** good – the best I've ever read!
11 We're **really / nearly** at the university. Go past the cinema and we're there.
12 Bob thinks **almost / a lot** about the poor children in Africa.
13 My grandfather doesn't like **new technology very much / very much new technology**.
14 Can you believe Roger is **almost an adult / nearly adult**?
15 Sophia did **well / good** in the cycling competition – I'm sure she won.

7 marks

3 Write the verbs in the present perfect tense or first conditional form.

LOOKING FORWARD TO THE FUTURE

Ebo Matata is a hip-hop singer from Zimbabwe. He (16) ___________ (**enter**) lots of music competitions. (17) ___________ (**you / ever be**) in a music competition and sung in front of a lot of people? It's not easy! Ebo (18) ___________ (**not win**) all of the competitions he's been in, but he has always done his best. This summer, he is going to the UK to sing at a huge hip-hop concert – his parents (19) ___________ (**give**) him their permission and his best friend Jo-Jo (20) ___________ (**buy**) him a plane ticket. Ebo hopes he sings well at the concert. If he (21) ___________ (**not sing**) well, he will be very upset. But Ebo knows that if he works hard, he (22) ___________ (**get**) better and better at what he does. He (23) ___________ (**practise**) a lot, so he'll do very well at the concert. Eventually, Ebo wants to be the best hip-hop singer in the world. He says that if he (24) ___________ (**be**) the best hip-hop singer in the world, he (25) ___________ (**earn**) a lot of money and be very famous.

10 marks

Total: ___ / 25 marks

Check your progress! | Units 1-14

1 Read the dialogue and choose the correct answer, A, B or C.

Jessica: Have you (1) ___ a job yet, Steve?
Steve: Yes, I saw an advert for a job in a newspaper. They're looking for a (2) ___ to write movie reviews and other articles.
Jessica: That's great!
Steve: Yes, it is. They just called me and I have an interview tomorrow morning. I'm quite (3) ___, you know – this is the first place I looked and it seems like a good job.
Jessica: Yes, I (4) ___. A newspaper is a great place to work. Well, I hope you (5) ___ them well.
Steve: Thanks. Me too. I'll let you know!

1 **A** picked up **B** gone past **C** applied for
2 **A** passenger **B** customer **C** reporter
3 **A** lucky **B** upset **C** angry
4 **A** nod **B** argue **C** agree
5 **A** welcome **B** get on with **C** grow up

5 marks

2 Write a word or phrase from the box in each gap. Some words and phrases will not be used.

allow • best friend • enjoy • lifetime • program • programme • relationship • scientist • uncle • whizz kid

My (6) __________ is Thomas Kale. He lives four houses down from me and we've known each other since we were both five. Our (7) __________ is very good. We never fight and we like many of the same things. We spend a lot of time together at the weekends and we (8) __________ ourselves playing computer games or playing football in the garden. Thomas also knows how to (9) __________ computers. He learned how to do it from his dad, who is a(n) (10) __________. Isn't that cool?

5 marks

3 Choose the correct answer.

While Mary (11) **was looking / looked** at her calendar yesterday, she (12) **was seeing / saw** that she had something very important to do – practise for her driving test next Monday. So she (13) **is going / goes** with her dad later today behind an empty shopping centre to practise for the test. She thinks it (14) **is / will be** very difficult. She (15) **never took / has never taken** a driving test before, so she's quite worried. She hopes that practising will help.

5 marks

4 Read the text and for each question, choose the correct answer, A, B or C.

If Martin goes to university next year, he (16) ___ to be a doctor. He really likes to help (17) ___ and he thinks being a doctor is the (18) ___ job for this. He knows doctors make (19) ___ money, but he doesn't want to do it for that reason. He believes it's (20) ___ important to do a job you're going to enjoy and not just think about money.

16 **A** study **B** will study **C** studies
17 **A** peoples **B** person **C** people
18 **A** good **B** better **C** best
19 **A** any **B** many **C** a lot of
20 **A** extremely **B** almost **C** very much

5 marks

5 Each of the words or phrases in bold is incorrect. Write the correct words on the lines.

21 You don't **must** to cook dinner tonight. I'll do it. __________
22 **When** did you put the milk? I can't find it. __________
23 That's **a** book I was telling you about. __________
24 We're meeting the director **at** 3rd April. __________
25 'Did you clean your room?' 'Yes, I **was**.' __________

5 marks

Total:____ / 25 marks

Answer key

Unit 1
This is Me!

Reading

Exercise 1
1 A 2 C 3 B 4 A 5 A 6 C

Wordpower!

Exercise 2
1 f 2 e 3 c 4 d 5 b 6 a

Exercise 3
1 country
2 only child
3 best
4 share
5 close
6 chat

Grammar 1

Exercise 1
1 ✓ 2 ✓ 5 ✓ 7 ✓

Exercise 2
1 is
2 am
3 have
4 got
5 Do
6 have
7 are
8 Have

Exercise 3
1 we're not
2 he does
3 she has
4 I don't
5 it hasn't
6 they are

Exercise 4
2 Beth and Marge don't have a TV.
3 Do you have a large house?
4 My cat doesn't have a name.
5 He hasn't got a computer.
6 I haven't got a lot of friends.
7 Has Sophia got a best friend?
8 Have they got a pet?

Wordpower!

Exercise 1
1 great-grandfather
2 nephew
3 grandfather
4 uncle
5 niece
6 cousins
7 grandmother
8 brother
9 great-grandmother
10 aunt

Exercise 2
1 B
2 A
3 B
4 B
5 A
6 B
7 A
8 A
9 A
10 B

Listening

Exercise 1
1 c 2 a 3 b

Exercise 2
1 thirteen
2 brother
3 sisters
4 Sheila
5 friends

Grammar 2

Exercise 1
1 mine / my
2 theirs / their
3 her / hers
4 your / ours
5 your / its
6 his / yours

Exercise 2
1 my
2 yours
3 his
4 her
5 its
6 ours
7 their
8 theirs

Exercise 3
1 B
2 A
3 C
4 B
5 A
6 B
7 B
8 B
9 C
10 B

Quick check

Exercise 4
1 yes
2 yes
3 no
4 is
5 both
6 before
7 adjectives
8 after the 's'

Writing

Exercise 1
1 I'm Zak and I'm twelve years old.
2 I'm quite tall and I've got brown hair.
3 My cousin's got blue eyes.
4 She doesn't have many friends.
5 No, I don't.
6 This is my favourite book – it's full of funny stories.

Unit 2
On the Farm!

Reading

Exercise 1
1 A 2 C 3 C 4 C 5 B

Wordpower!

Exercise 2
1 feed
2 pick
3 plants
4 touch
5 welcome
6 stroke
7 collects
8 moves

Exercise 3
1 B
2 A
3 C
4 A
5 C
6 B
7 C
8 C

Grammar 1

Exercise 1
1 work
2 doesn't live
3 Do you want
4 goes
5 Does Ned like
6 don't wake up
7 get up
8 Do they visit

Exercise 2
1 Visitors leave the farm in the evening.
2 Lisa plays with the puppies every day.
3 Sally and I don't work a lot on the farm.
4 Does your day start at 7am?
5 I love Ned the donkey.
6 Do Peter and Joe live on the farm all year?
7 The children see the calves in the afternoon.
8 She doesn't eat eggs for breakfast.

Exercise 3
1 doesn't
2 Do students
3 arrive
4 Does
5 takes
6 don't
7 Do
8 don't

Exercise 4
1 lives
2 like
3 feed
4 visit
5 play
6 don't
7 doesn't
8 go
9 run
10 don't

Wordpower!

Exercise 1
1 minutes
2 past
3 hours
4 seconds
5 o'clock
6 quarter
7 watch

Exercise 2
1 o'clock
2 half
3 an hour
4 to
5 minutes
6 seconds
7 watch

Listening

Exercise 1
1 B 2 A 3 B

Exercise 2
1 Waltham
2 10 o'clock
3 sheep
4 one o'clock
5 half past four

Grammar 2

Exercise 1
1 The Collins visit the city every week.
2 Frank is usually tired at the end of the day.
3 Do you ride horses every day?
4 Susan is never late to feed the animals.
5 Does Dad always get up at five o'clock?
6 I am often busy in the mornings.

Exercise 2
1 <u>never</u>, I never wake up early in the morning.
2 <u>every year</u>, We pick vegetables at this time every year.
3 ✓
4 <u>often</u>, The cows often eat all of their food.
5 <u>always</u>, Mary always arrives late to the farm.
6 <u>every day</u>, Mum cooks lunch for us every day.

Exercise 3
1 C
2 B
3 B
4 C
5 B
6 A
7 C
8 C
9 A
10 C

Quick check

Exercise 4

1 yes
2 They live on a farm.
3 Does Sam feed the cows?
4 no
5 My dog is often happy.
6 both

Writing

Exercise 1

2 We wake up at seven. Then we help our dad with work.
3 After we have breakfast, we pick fruit and vegetables.
4 We have lunch at one. Then we ride horses.
5 After we walk the ponies, we go home.

Exercise 2

1 G 5 F
2 C 6 D
3 A 7 B
4 E

Check your Progress! | Units 1–2

Exercise 1

1 country 5 collect
2 cousins 6 plant
3 grandmother 7 best
4 feed

Exercise 2

8 I have two close friends.
9 My cousin is in the girls' room.
10 Does Sheila feed the animals every day?
11 Are you an only child?
12 Is your mother often late?
13 Where's Peter's niece?
14 They never go to the city.
15 They don't live in the country.

Exercise 3

16 Do you plant fruit and vegetables? / Do you plant vegetables and fruit?
17 He hasn't got a best friend.
18 Look in her bedroom.
19 Have Sacha and Wendy got a dog?
20 They love visiting the farm.
21 That pony is mine.
22 Bob has lunch every day.
23 Give the kitten its dinner.
24 Is your grandfather often tired?
25 We don't brush the ponies in the morning.

Unit 3
Going Shopping!

Reading

Exercise 1

1 b 2 c 3 d

Exercise 2

1 her cousin
2 funny puppies
3 hungry and tired
4 socks
5 the girl's mum
6 flowers

Wordpower!

Exercise 3

1 A 4 C
2 C 5 B
3 B 6 A

Exercise 4

1 busy 2 customers 3 enjoying 4 getting
5 escalator 6 lift 7 expensive 8 cheap

Grammar 1

Exercise 1

1 They are having lunch now.
2 I'm not feeling tired.
3 Are they enjoying their dinner?
4 'No, he isn't.'
5 Is he looking for clothes?
6 She's picking a flower.
7 We are not shopping at the moment.
8 'Yes, I am.'

Exercise 2

1 Are you feeling bored?
2 We are playing a computer game.
3 It's not eating its dinner.
4 I am collecting eggs.
5 They are not doing their homework now.
6 Is he shopping at the grocer's?

Exercise 3

2 Are you watching TV now?
You aren't watching TV now.
3 Is he out shopping right now?
He isn't out shopping right now.
4 Are they feeling unhappy?
They aren't feeling unhappy.
5 Are we having a sale right now?
We aren't having a sale right now.
6 Is Marta looking for new shoes?
Marta isn't looking for new shoes.

Exercise 4
1 you're not
2 I am
3 he is
4 they aren't
5 we / you aren't
6 she is

Wordpower!

Exercise 1
1 tiny
2 circular
3 thin
4 huge
5 square, flat
6 rectangular
7 large
8 gigantic

Listening

Exercise 1
1 F
2 F
3 T
4 T
5 T
6 F

Exercise 2
1 cousin's
2 week
3 pink
4 shoes
5 fifteen
6 ten

Grammar 2

Exercise 1
1 myself
2 yourself
3 yourselves
4 himself
5 herself
6 itself
7 ourselves
8 themselves

Exercise 2
1 this, that
2 these, those
3 these, those
4 that, this

Exercise 3
1 B
2 A
3 C
4 C
5 A
6 B
7 A
8 A
9 B
10 A

Quick check

Exercise 4
1 yes
2 yes
3 both
4 He's shopping now.
5 pronoun
6 ourselves
7 no
8 I need that book over there.

Writing

Exercise 1
1 socks 2 skirts 3 yes 4 no

Exercise 2
1 are having
2 are going
3 are looking
4 is wearing
5 is looking
6 is buying
7 is getting
8 are enjoying
9 is feeling
10 isn't having

Unit 4
Read All About It!

Reading

Exercise 1
1 A
2 B
3 B
4 A
5 B
6 C
7 B
8 C

Wordpower!

Exercise 2
1 editor
2 reporter
3 calendar
4 interview
5 opinion
6 review

Exercise 3
1 b
2 d
3 c
4 f
5 a
6 e

Exercise 4
1 B
2 A
3 C
4 B
5 A
6 B

Grammar 1

Exercise 1
1 When
2 Which
3 How many
4 Who
5 Why
6 What

Exercise 2
1 many, old
2 Where, Which
3 old, time
4 ✓
5 Who, Where
6 ✓

Exercise 3
2 When do you go to school?
3 How old are you?
4 How many sisters have you got?
5 Where do you live?
6 What do you read?

Exercise 4
1 how
2 where
3 what
4 which
5 why
6 who

Wordpower!

Exercise 1
1 speak
2 lie
3 whisper
4 talk
5 shout
6 scream
7 tell, time

Exercise 2

1 speak
2 say
3 talk
4 lie
5 telling
6 shout
7 screams
8 whispers
9 talk

Listening

Exercise 1

1 school play
2 on a website
3 Thomas

Exercise 2

1 B
2 A
3 C
4 A
5 B

Grammar 2

Exercise 1

1 too, very
2 ✓
3 ✓
4 too, very
5 ✓
6 too, very

Exercise 2

2 Mrs Niles is too old to ski.
3 The article's too short to use.
4 She's too young to have a car.
5 Evan writes too badly to read his work.
6 It's too early to go to bed.

Exercise 3

1 too
2 well
3 very
4 for me to
5 good
6 very
7 quickly
8 too

Quick check

Exercise 4

1 no
2 Where do you live?
3 Who's your maths teacher?
4 yes
5 no
6 This article's very long but I like it.

Writing

Exercise 1

1 f
2 d
3 g
4 e
5 a
6 h
7 c
8 b

Exercise 2

2 Fifteen.
3 Because it's lovely.
4 At eight o'clock.
5 This spring.
6 *The Game*.

Check your Progress! | Units 3-4

Exercise 1

1 C
2 B
3 C
4 A
5 C
6 C
7 B
8 A
9 C

Exercise 2

10 are going
11 are/'re walking
12 is/'s eating
13 am/'m wearing
14 are/'re having
15 are/'re turning
16 is/'s standing
17 is/'s waving

Exercise 3

18 herself
19 them
20 they
21 mine
22 How many
23 Why
24 How
25 very

Unit 5
The Travel Bug!

Reading

Exercise 1

1 B 2 B 3 A 4 B

Exercise 2

1 T
2 T
3 F
4 F
5 T
6 F
7 T
8 F
9 T
10 T

Wordpower!

Exercise 3

1 tourists
2 sights
3 traffic
4 capital
5 tickets
6 view
7 guide
8 trip
9 tour

Exercise 4

1 sights
2 traffic
3 tourists
4 guide
5 trip
6 tickets
7 capital
8 view
9 tour

Grammar 1

Exercise 1

1 was / were
2 came
3 gave
4 got
5 went
6 had
7 made
8 saw
9 took
10 did

Exercise 2

1 a	6 j
2 d	7 g
3 h	8 b
4 f	9 c
5 e	10 i

Exercise 3

1 came	6 saw
2 gave	7 took
3 gives	8 went
4 was	9 had
5 got	10 made

Exercise 4

1 this morning	4 last week
2 yesterday	5 this morning
3 this afternoon	6 last night

Wordpower!

Exercise 1

Africa:	Egypt, Kenya, Zimbabwe
Asia:	China, India, Japan, Oman, Qatar, Russia, Turkey, Yemen
Europe:	Austria, Denmark, France, Georgia, Hungary, Latvia, Norway, Poland, Russia, Spain, Turkey, Ukraine, Wales
North America:	Mexico
South America:	Brazil, Venezuela

Listening

Exercise 1

1 B	3 A	5 C
2 C	4 B	6 A

Exercise 2

1 View	4 Road
2 ninety	5 sights
3 city	

Grammar 2

Exercise 1

1 f	7 h
2 a	8 b
3 k	9 e
4 c	10 g
5 j	11 i
6 d	

Exercise 2

1 visited	5 didn't visit
2 did	6 didn't eat
3 told	7 wrote
4 begin	8 Did he visit

Exercise 3

1 drove	5 flew
2 found	6 told
3 left	7 met
4 ate	8 began

Exercise 4

1 B	6 B
2 A	7 B
3 C	8 A
4 C	9 A
5 A	10 C

Quick check

Exercise 5

1 yes
2 yes
3 They were there yesterday.
4 Did Mum make this?
5 came
6 Did you begin your trip yesterday?
7 now
8 No, I didn't.

Writing

Exercise 1

1 B 2 A 3 C

Exercise 2

Hello, Dominic!
California is fantastic! Last week, we drove from New York to California. We were in our tiny car for hours every day – it was so boring – and every night I was very tired. But now we're here and I am happy and very excited! America is a gigantic country and California is huge. It's very hot here now, but not too hot – I don't mind this weather, I think it's great. Our hotel is amazing. It has got a big, circular swimming pool – I go swimming a lot. I also eat a lot! The meals here at the hotel are delicious. My dad said they were expensive, but Mum told me they were cheap.
See you soon,
Giselle

Unit 6
Animal Magic!

Reading

Exercise 1

1 B 2 C 3 C

Exercise 2

1 brown	4 winter
2 brother	5 dog
3 puppies	6 interesting

Wordpower!

Exercise 3

1 f 2 b 3 c 4 a 5 e 6 d

Exercise 4

1 C 2 A 3 B 4 C 5 C

Exercise 5
1 memory 4 sweet
2 lifetime 5 grow
3 lick 6 fact

Grammar 1

Exercise 1
1 leg, legs 4 sheeps, sheep
2 child, children 5 box, boxes
3 ✓ 6 cherry, cherries

Exercise 2
1 men 4 adults
2 babies 5 women
3 kittens 6 humans

Exercise 3
1 Mice have got four feet.
2 Crocodiles have got 70 teeth.
3 Goldfish have got good memories.
4 Puppies have got cute faces.
5 Flies have got small mouths.
6 Many animals have got tongues.

Exercise 4
1 butterflies 4 sizes
2 gardens 5 countries
3 colours 6 days

Wordpower!

Exercise 1
1 pick 5 walk
2 push 6 jump
3 drop 7 put
4 run 8 pull

Exercise 2
1 C 2 B 3 A 4 C 5 B 6 B 7 A 8 C

Listening

Exercise 1
1 B 2 A 3 B 4 A

Exercise 2
1 b 2 d 3 c 4 e 5 f

Grammar 2

Exercise 1
1 A gecko is an interesting pet.
2 An aye-aye is a strange animal.
3 There is an adult giraffe at the zoo.
4 Is there a small elephant at the park?
5 There's an enormous python in the garden!
6 Is an African lion on TV?

Exercise 2
1 the 6 –
2 the 7 the
3 – 8 –
4 – 9 –
5 the 10 –

Exercise 3
1 C 5 C 9 B
2 B 6 C 10 A
3 B 7 C 11 A
4 A 8 B 12 C

Quick check

Exercise 4
1 no 4 yes
2 both 5 no
3 both 6 Today is 15th April.

Writing

Exercise 1
1 B 2 A 3 B 4 A 5 B

Exercise 2
1 Feed the dogs twice a day.
2 Play with the cat for twenty minutes.
3 Don't let the lizard out of his cage.
4 Make sure there's lots of water.
5 Don't forget to put the food away.

Check your Progress! | Units 5–6

Exercise 1
1 Africa 5 facts
2 Zimbabwe 6 lick
3 trip 7 lifetime
4 sights

Exercise 2
8 children 12 an
9 the 13 –
10 – 14 cherries
11 mice 15 teeth

Exercise 3
16 Did Mum and Dad fly to India last week? Mum and Dad didn't fly to India last week.
17 Were you and Tom late for the tour this morning? You and Tom weren't late for the tour this morning.
18 Did you make hot dogs for dinner last night? You didn't make hot dogs for dinner last night.
19 Did Hans and Peter go to visit Times Square at 5 o'clock? Hans and Peter didn't go to visit Times Square at 5 o'clock.
20 Was Betty in the capital city of the USA this summer? Betty wasn't in the capital city of the USA this summer.

Unit 7
At the Airport!

Reading

Exercise 1
1 c 2 a, f 3 b 4 d, g

Exercise 2
1 a pilot
2 a reporter
3 during the flight
4 a/the mechanic
5 a/the passport
6 a scanner

Wordpower!

Exercise 3
1 catch
2 takes off
3 passengers
4 safe
5 passport
6 baggage
7 emergency
8 landing

Exercise 4
1 B 2 A 3 A 4 B 5 A 6 B 7 B 8 A

Grammar 1

Exercise 1
1 C 2 C 3 C 4 U 5 C 6 C 7 U 8 U 9 U
10 C 11 U 12 C 13 U 14 U 15 C 16 C

Exercise 2
1 travels
2 a hair
3 time
4 hair
5 a coffee
6 times
7 coffee
8 travel

Exercise 3
1 C 2 A 3 C 4 C 5 A 6 B 7 B 8 A
9 C 10 A

Wordpower!

Exercise 1
1 cardboard, cotton
2 metal, wood
3 leather, cotton
4 plastic, glass
5 rubber, glass

Exercise 2
1 plastic
2 metal
3 glass
4 leather
5 cotton
6 cardboard

Listening

Exercise 1
1 c 2 a 3 b

Exercise 2
1 Egypt
2 passengers
3 two
4 sixth
5 grandmother

Grammar 2

Exercise 1
1 B 2 A 3 A 4 B 5 A 6 B

Exercise 2
1 some/no
2 no/some
3 any
4 any
5 a lot of/many
6 many/a lot of
7 a lot of/much
8 much/a lot of

Exercise 3
1 lot
2 some
3 any
4 much
5 some
6 any
7 many
8 no
9 some
10 any

Quick check

Exercise 4
1 yes
2 yes
3 both
4 is
5 some
6 both
7 both
8 much

Writing

Exercise 1
1 In the foreground
2 In the background
3 On the right
4 On the left

Exercise 2
1 B 2 C

Unit 8
Lucky Escapes!

Reading

Exercise 1
1 C 2 C 3 C 4 C 5 B

Exercise 2
1 d 2 e 3 b 4 c 5 a

Wordpower!

Exercise 3
1 upset
2 knocked
3 crash
4 get out
5 successful
6 lucky
7 escape
8 extremely

Exercise 4
1 crash
2 lucky
3 upset
4 getting out
5 successful
6 knocked
7 escape
8 extremely

Grammar 1

Exercise 1

1 were watching
2 was riding
3 was sailing
4 were cooking
5 weren't travelling
6 was laughing
7 were driving
8 weren't playing

Exercise 2

1 got
2 were filming
3 were fishing
4 came
5 was driving
6 turned

Exercise 3

1 played, were playing
2 was answering, answered
3 ✓
4 rode, was riding
5 was seeing, saw
6 ran, was running

Exercise 4

1 B 2 C 3 B 4 C 5 A 6 C 7 A 8 B 9 C 10 B

Wordpower!

Exercise 1

1 shake
2 nod
3 kiss
4 wave
5 point
6 shake

Exercise 2

1 wave
2 shaking
3 pointing
4 nodding
5 shake
6 Kiss

Listening

Exercise 1

1 F 2 F 3 T 4 F 5 F 6 T

Exercise 2

1 France
2 night
3 sister
4 window
5 interesting
6 sun

Grammar 2

Exercise 1

1 was
2 didn't
3 can
4 wasn't
5 am
6 did
7 weren't
8 have

Exercise 2

1 Yes, I did.
2 Yes, she was.
3 Yes, I was.
4 No, I'm not.
5 Yes, we can.
6 Yes, I do.
7 No, I haven't.
8 No, we shouldn't.

Exercise 3

1 Were
2 was
3 I
4 he
5 was
6 can't
7 were
8 didn't
9 there
10 was

Quick check

Exercise 4

1 yes
2 yes
3 She was working when I called.
4 yes
5 no
6 Yes, we do.

Writing

Exercise 1

1 3 2 5 3 6 4 4 5 2 6 1

Exercise 2

1 at the weekend
2 writer's friend
3 close to the front
4 Jessica
5 The writer and her friends
6 funny

Check your Progress! | Units 7-8

Exercise 1

1 landed
2 upset
3 passport
4 shake
5 lucky
6 baggage
7 metal
8 passenger
9 extremely
10 took off

Exercise 2

11 were walking
12 saw
13 was driving
14 ran
15 didn't have
16 hit
17 wasn't going
18 knocked

Exercise 3

19 B 20 C 21 C 22 C 23 A 24 B 25 C

Unit 9
Friends and Family!

Reading

Exercise 1

1 B 2 A 3 A

Exercise 2

1 yes
2 yes
3 no
4 no
5 no
6 no
7 yes
8 yes
9 no
10 yes

Wordpower!

Exercise 3

1 give
2 fair
3 let
4 argue
5 allow
6 Grow
7 get
8 relationship

Exercise 4

1 let
2 permission
3 grow
4 fair
5 relationship
6 get
7 argue
8 allow

Grammar 1

Exercise 1

2 ✓ 3 ✓ 6 ✓ 8 ✓ 9 ✓

Exercise 2

1 can
2 can't
3 could
4 couldn't
5 can
6 can't
7 can't
8 Can
9 can't
10 Could

Exercise 3

2 Could Ivan speak three languages when he was five?
Ivan couldn't speak three languages when he was five.

3 Could we help you with that?
We couldn't help you with that.

4 Can they take us to the restaurant?
They can't take us to the restaurant.

5 Could you come with us?
You couldn't come with us.

6 Can Marta drive a car?
Marta can't drive a car.

Exercise 4

1 you can't
2 he could
3 you could
4 they can't
5 I/we couldn't
6 she can

Wordpower!

Exercise 1

1 upset
2 angry
3 worried
4 surprised
5 confused
6 scared

Exercise 2

1 angry
2 upset
3 confused
4 scared
5 surprised
6 worried

Listening

Exercise 1

1 T 2 T 3 T 4 F 5 F 6 F 7 T 8 F

Exercise 2

1 party
2 June
3 Lucky's
4 Airport
5 midnight

Grammar 2

Exercise 1

1 I shouldn't go to the cinema.
2 No, he doesn't.
3 We don't have to get tickets.
4 You shouldn't shout all the time.
5 Yes, you do.
6 You have to try harder.
7 Yes, she does.
8 You can come to the party, but you don't have to.

Exercise 2

2 We don't have to clean our room.
3 You mustn't cry.
4 Your friend must talk to you.
5 Should I ask the teacher?
6 Sophia has to empty the bins.
7 We have to ask for permission.
8 You shouldn't get angry.
9 You should say you're sorry.
10 We must promise to help.

Exercise 3

1 f 2 e 3 d 4 g 5 b

Quick check

Exercise 4

1 yes
2 yes
3 Could you talk to her?
4 You can't go.
5 no
6 no
7 yes
8 yes

Writing

Exercise 1

All of us <u>have to</u> help around the house. Yes, that means you too, Frannie! Duke, you <u>don't have to</u> help because you're a dog.

On Mondays, Wednesdays and Fridays, Frannie <u>has to</u> do the washing up and Hans, <u>has to</u> empty the bins. Hans you <u>mustn't</u> forget the bin in your room.

Mum <u>must</u> cook lunch and dinner on Saturdays and Sundays. Dad <u>must</u> cook dinner on week days. He <u>can</u> buy pizzas on really busy days.

Hans <u>has to</u> feed Duke every morning and give him water. Frannie <u>has to</u> feed him every night. She <u>should</u> do it before 6pm or he gets upset. Hans, <u>could</u> you feed Duke for Frannie on the days she gets back late from football matches, please?

These are the new rules. I <u>couldn't</u> think of any others. You <u>can</u> talk to me or Mum about them. You <u>shouldn't</u> shout or cry when you talk to us about them. Be mature – we <u>can</u> solve any problems together!

Exercise 2
present/past ability
1 couldn't
give permission
2 can
3 can
4 can
make polite requests
5 could
obligation
6 have to
7 has to
8 has to
9 mustn't
10 must
11 must
12 has to
13 has to
lack of obligation
14 don't have to
give advice
15 should
16 shouldn't

Unit 10
Being the Best!

Reading

Exercise 1
1 A 2 B 3 C 4 A 5 B 6 B 7 A 8 B

Wordpower!

Exercise 2
1 eventually
2 certain
3 competition
4 agrees
5 discovers
6 by mistake
7 gives up
8 right

Exercise 3
1 competition
2 right
3 give up
4 discover
5 eventually
6 certain
7 agree
8 by mistake

Grammar 1

Exercise 1
1 better
2 stronger
3 taller
4 smaller
5 more interesting
6 larger
7 more comfortable
8 younger

Exercise 2
1 faster, slower
2 happier, sadder
3 more difficult, easier
4 colder, hotter

Exercise 3
1 quicker
2 faster
3 shorter
4 better
5 cleaner
6 nicer
7 more enjoyable
8 smarter

Exercise 4
2 A mouse is weaker than an elephant.
3 Maths is not harder than history.
4 Running is more boring than swimming.
5 A lion is scarier than a mouse.
6 Stephen is angrier than George.

Wordpower!

Exercise 1
1 heavy
2 thin
3 fat
4 dark
5 light
6 slim
7 fair
8 light

Exercise 2
1 B 2 C 3 A 4 A 5 B 6 C 7 B 8 A

Listening

Exercise 1
1 A 2 A 3 B 4 B

Exercise 2
1 more interesting
2 doesn't agree
3 more boring
4 Science
5 English
6 maths and science

Grammar 2

Exercise 1
1 dangerous
2 tallest
3 highest
4 fastest
5 worst
6 best

Exercise 2
1 Eric is the slimmest person in my family.
2 Mary has got the longest hair in school.
3 Basketball is the most enjoyable sport.
4 Which chair is the most comfortable chair in your house?
5 Elephants are the heaviest animals in this zoo.
6 Chess is the most interesting game in the world.

Exercise 3
1 C 2 B 3 C 4 A 5 C 6 B 7 A 8 B 9 C 10 B
11 C 12 A

Quick check

Exercise 4
1 no
2 no
3 both
4 yes
5 yes
6 both

Writing

Exercise 1

1 ✓ 2 ✓ 3 X 4 ✓ 5 X 6 ✓ 7 ✓ 8 ✓

Exercise 2

2 Lisa is not as fast as Nicole.
3 Maths is not as interesting as history.
4 Football is not as hard as basketball.
5 Mr Peters is not as nice as Mrs Johnson.
6 The chair is not as comfortable as the sofa.

Check your Progress! | Units 9-10

Exercise 1

1 permission
2 allow
3 worried
4 certain
5 dark
6 competition
7 fair

Exercise 2

8 faster, quicker
9 could, can
10 shouldn't, the rudest
11 must, have to

Exercise 3

12 B 13 A 14 C 15 C 16 A 17 B 18 B 19 A 20 C 21 A

Unit 11
Planning for Tomorrow!

Reading

Exercise 1

1 C 2 B 3 A 4 A 5 C 6 A 7 C 8 A 9 A

Exercise 2

1 thirteen
2 play football
3 the UK
4 four or five
5 four
6 five or six

Wordpower!

Exercise 3

1 sure
2 kid
3 guess
4 school
5 program
6 company
7 app
8 play

Exercise 4

1 sure
2 school
3 play
4 guess
5 company
6 kid
7 program
8 apps

Grammar 1

Exercise 1

1 Are you going to go
2 is not going to appear
3 Is he going to practise
4 am not going to see
5 is going to be
6 are going to get
7 Am I going to develop
8 am going to study
9 are not going to work
10 are going to visit

Exercise 2

1 is going to feed
2 is going to brush
3 is going to let
4 are going to plant
5 is going to move
6 is going to collect
7 is going to ride
8 is going to pick

Exercise 3

2 Are you going to work with computers?
No, you're not.
Are you going to be famous and successful?
Yes, you are.
3 Is Ivan going to work with computers?
No, he isn't.
Is Ivan going to be famous and successful?
Yes, he is.
4 Is Marta going to work with computers?
Yes, she is.
Is Marta going to be famous and successful?
No, she isn't.
5 Are Sven and Hans going to work with computers?
No, they aren't.
Are Sven and Hans going to be famous and successful?
Yes, they are.
6 Are Brendon and I going to work with computers?
No, we aren't.
Are Brendon and I going to be famous and successful?
Yes, we are.

Wordpower!

Exercise 1

2 all of
3 half of
4 a third of
5 almost all of
6 almost half of
7 a quarter of
8 none of

Exercise 2

1 All of
2 None of
3 most of
4 A quarter of
5 A third of
6 Almost half of
7 Almost all of
8 Half of

Listening

Exercise 1

1 g 2 d 3 a 4 f 5 b 6 e

Exercise 2

1 F 2 T 3 T 4 T 5 F 6 F

Grammar 2

Exercise 1

1 F 2 I 3 P 4 F 5 P 6 I

Exercise 2
1 f 2 b 3 c 4 g 5 d 6 e 7 h 8 a

Exercise 3
2 What time will you go to Jane's party on Friday night?
 ... I will go at eight o'clock.
3 What will she wear to school tomorrow?
 ... she will wear a skirt and a T-shirt.
4 What will I see on the farm at the weekend?
 ... you will see lambs and chicks.
5 What job will Petros have when he's thirty?
 ... he will be a pilot.
6 What will they do on holiday?
 ... they will do nothing special on holiday.

Quick check

Exercise 4
1 both
2 no
3 They're going to travel to Kenya.
4 both
5 yes
6 yes
7 yes
8 He'll be a successful adult.

Writing

Exercise 1
1 c 2 e 3 d 4 a 5 b

Exercise 2
1 ✓ 3 ✓ 4 ✓ 5 ✓

Unit 12
Lights! Camera! Action!

Reading

Exercise 1
1 d 2 c 3 e 4 b 5 a

Exercise 2
1 T 2 F 3 F 4 T 5 F 6 F

Wordpower!

Exercise 3
1 movies
2 prepare
3 empty
4 role
5 shoot
6 action movie
7 in the background
8 scene

Exercise 4
1 movie
2 action
3 role
4 prepare
5 scene
6 shoot
7 background
8 empty

Grammar 1

Exercise 1
1 is/'s preparing
2 are/'re doing
3 am/'m getting
4 are/'re shooting
5 is/'s taking
6 are/'re not giving

Exercise 2
1 am/'m going
2 are/'re not meeting
3 is/'s playing
4 are/'re having
5 are/'re shooting
6 am/'m not trying on

Exercise 3
1 am/'m arriving
2 are/'re shooting
3 are/'re leaving
4 are/'re visiting
5 are/'re putting on
6 are/'re preparing
7 are/'re having
8 are/'re changing
9 are/'re not preparing
10 are/'re playing
11 are/'re starting
12 are/'re finishing

Wordpower!

Exercise 1
1 mountain
2 cliff
3 desert
4 field
5 beach
6 forest
7 lake

Exercise 2
1 beach
2 cliff
3 mountain
4 lake
5 field
6 desert
7 forest

Listening

Exercise 1
1 g 2 d 3 f 4 a 5 c 6 h

Exercise 2
1 C 2 A 3 C 4 B 5 B 6 A

Grammar 2

Exercise 1
1 e 2 h 3 a 4 f 5 c 6 d 7 g 8 b

Exercise 2
1 near 2 on 3 at 4 into 5 by 6 for

Exercise 3
1 C 2 A 3 C 4 C 5 C 6 A 7 A 8 C 9 B 10 B
11 A 12 B 13 C 14 A 15 C

Quick check

Exercise 4
1 yes
2 no
3 What are you doing tonight?
4 yes
5 yes
6 I'm at home.

Writing

Exercise 1

2 f 3 b 4 a 5 e 6 c

Exercise 2

1 story
2 say
3 scenes
4 film reviews
5 action movie
6 nine months

Check your Progress! | Units 11-12

Exercise 1

1 C 2 C 3 B 4 C 5 C 6 B 7 A 8 C 9 B 10 C

Exercise 2

11 I'm going to wear my jacket tomorrow.
12 Are you going to travel to Spain next week?
13 Rachel is going to practise music tonight.
14 Are we going to study for the maths test later?
15 Ben and Steve are going to play football this weekend.

Exercise 3

16 Will the classes be difficult?
17 Jake will enjoy the gift very much.
18 I will not/won't go to university in the summer.
19 Will it be hot in Greece?
20 We will/'ll do well on our exams.

Exercise 4

21 Are
22 playing
23 They are not
24 at 9pm on Wednesday
25 at home on 4th April

Unit 13
Raising Money!

Reading

Exercise 1

1 B 2 A 3 C 4 C

Exercise 2

1 ✓ 3 ✓ 5 ✓ 6 ✓ 7 ✓

Wordpower!

Exercise 3

1 enter
2 poor
3 raise
4 rich
5 charity
6 messy
7 local
8 marathon

Exercise 4

1 rich
2 poor
3 enter
4 raise
5 local
6 messy
7 charity

Grammar 1

Exercise 1

1 given
2 ever seen
3 flown
4 have been
5 Have we raised
6 never visited
7 you've
8 ever

Exercise 2

2 She has made lots of cakes.
3 He has sold fifty tickets.
4 They have gone to the local shops.
5 It has given us twenty new books.
6 We have brought old clothes to sell.

Exercise 3

2 She hasn't made lots of cakes.
3 He hasn't sold fifty tickets.
4 They haven't gone to the local shops.
5 It hasn't given us twenty new books.
6 We haven't brought old clothes to sell.

Exercise 4

1 have worked
2 have saved
3 have been
4 have given
5 has done
6 Have you ever helped
7 hasn't had
8 have entered
9 have asked
10 Has anyone told
11 has put
12 haven't done

Wordpower!

Exercise 1

1 T 2 F 3 T 4 T 5 T 6 T 7 F 8 T

Exercise 2

1 over
2 behind
3 top
4 above
5 underneath
6 beside
7 between
8 Below

Listening

Exercise 1

1 A 2 C 3 A 4 B 5 A 6 C

Exercise 2

1 Feed
2 14th
3 5
4 fifty
5 three hundred euros

Grammar 2

Exercise 1

1 carefully
2 successfully
3 quickly
4 loudly
5 nervously
6 well
7 easily
8 hard
9 safely
10 fast

Exercise 2

1 Why are you eating so fast?
2 Tanya whispered quietly to her best friend.
3 My mum makes cakes very well.
4 Our team won the match easily.
5 The little girl stroked the lamb gently.
6 Grandma sang happily in the garden.
7 Gerrard tried hard, but wasn't successful.
8 Bob plays the piano very badly.

Quick check

Exercise 3

1 no
2 yes
3 yes
4 Have you ever run in a marathon?
5 yes
6 My sister cooks very well.

Writing

Exercise 1

1 C 2 A 3 A

Exercise 2

December 14th

Doing my bit for charity!

Hi, everyone, welcome back. Today, I'm going to tell you about what my school did to raise money for the charity *WWF* on Saturday.

My school has raised money for charity <u>successfully</u> lots of times. One year, we had a concert and the money from the tickets helped build a school in Africa. Another time, we had a Market Day where we sold things to raise money. This year, the school decided to do something we've never done before – we had a hot-dog-eating marathon!

Students had to eat lots and lots of hot dogs, and they had to eat them <u>fast</u>! I had a plan; I ate the hot dogs <u>slowly</u> at first, but then, after two or three, I ate really <u>fast</u>. Some of the students did <u>well</u>, but I won the marathon <u>easily</u>. I ate eight hot dogs in five minutes and raised over fifty euros for charity! I didn't do <u>badly</u>, did I? Have you ever raised money for charity? Leave a comment below.

Unit 14
Looking Ahead!

Reading

Exercise 1

1 S 2 K 3 D 4 S 5 D 6 K

Exercise 2

1 twenty-three
2 scientist
3 moon
4 journey
5 role
6 faster

Wordpower!

Exercise 3

1 licence
2 university
3 universe
4 technology
5 predictions
6 apply for
7 scientist
8 move

Exercise 4

1 university
2 scientist
3 move
4 licence
5 apply for
6 universe
7 prediction

Grammar 1

Exercise 1

1 <u>I'll</u>, I
2 <u>don't</u>, won't
3 <u>you'll</u>, you
4 <u>hate</u>, will hate
5 <u>you'll</u>, you
6 ✓
7 <u>they'll</u>, they
8 ✓

Exercise 2

1 will meet
2 I'll
3 won't
4 we'll
5 will change
6 I

Exercise 3

2 We'll call you if we get lost.
3 If they meet, they'll like each other.
4 I'll give you this phone if I get a new one.
5 If you see this movie, you'll love it.
6 Life will be easier if technology improves.

Exercise 4

1 C 2 A 3 C 4 C 5 B 6 B 7 B 8 C

Wordpower!

Exercise 1

1 turn
2 go
3 Turn
4 go
5 turn
6 cross
7 turn
8 go

Exercise 2

1 C 2 B 3 C 4 A 5 B 6 C 7 A 8 B

Listening

Exercise 1

1 c 2 a 3 e 4 b 5 d

Exercise 2

1 East Road
2 Market Street
3 10 minutes
4 police station
5 turned back

Grammar 2

Exercise 1
1 B 2 B 3 A 4 B 5 A 6 A 7 B 8 A

Exercise 2
1 She's a really nice doctor.
2 You upset me a lot.
3 They're quite good at maths.
4 The desert is an extremely hot place.
5 I don't like science very much.
6 She almost lost her bags.
7 He's very good at his job.
8 I nearly forgot to do my homework.

Exercise 3
1 extremely
2 much
3 quite
4 nearly
5 lot
6 really

Quick check

Exercise 4
1 no
2 no
3 both
4 yes
5 yes
6 both

Writing

Exercise 1
1 B 2 B 3 A 4 B 5 A 6 B

Exercise 2
1 I will probably be rich someday.
2 When I get older, I might change jobs.
3 Maybe I'll be a famous singer.
4 I may give some money to poor people.
5 Perhaps I'll build nice places to work.

Check your Progress! | Units 13-14

Exercise 1
1 B 2 A 3 A 4 B 5 B 6 A 7 A 8 B

Exercise 2
9 loudly
10 extremely
11 nearly
12 a lot
13 new technology very much
14 almost an adult
15 well

Exercise 3
16 has entered
17 Have you ever been
18 hasn't won
19 have given
20 has bought
21 doesn't sing
22 will get
23 has practised
24 is
25 will earn

Check your Progress! | Units 1-14

Exercise 1
1 C 2 C 3 A 4 C 5 B

Exercise 2
6 best friend
7 relationship
8 enjoy
9 program
10 scientist

Exercise 3
11 was looking
12 saw
13 is going
14 will be
15 has never taken

Exercise 4
16 B 17 C 18 C 19 C 20 A

Exercise 5
21 have
22 Where
23 the
24 on
25 did

Audioscripts

Unit 1 Listening

Speaker 1: Hello, I'm Manu. I'm thirteen years old. My mum and dad, my brother Wafi and I live in India. I'm in Year 8 at school and I've got lots of friends. My best friend is Emir. We love playing computer games together, and playing with his cat, Boots. My mum doesn't like pets, so I don't have one.

Speaker 2: Hi. My name is Eileen. I'm twelve and I live in Leeds. I've got a very noisy house! I have three brothers and three sisters and a lot of cousins. I also have a cat. Her name is Jo-Jo. My best friend's name is Sheila. She's got a beautiful house in the country and we spend a lot of time there.

Speaker 3: Hello. My name is Miguel. I'm from Spain and I'm eleven. I haven't got any brothers or sisters but I'm not lonely. I have two close friends and I have a best friend – my dog, Prince! Prince and I spend a lot of time at my grandparent's house in the country.

Unit 2 Listening

Woman: Chester Farms, how may I help you?

Man: Hello. I would like to visit your farm this weekend and I'd like to know some things.

Woman: Sure, what would you like to know?

Man: Can you tell me where Chester Farms is?

Woman: Of course. We're just outside the town of Waltham. That's W-A-L-T-H-A-M. The farm is on Chester Road. There's a sign in town, so it's easy to find.

Man: And what time do visitors arrive at the farm?

Woman: We open at 10 o'clock every day.

Man: Great. What kinds of animals have you got on the farm?

Woman: Well, we make milk on the farm, so we've got lots of cows. We've also got horses and sheep.

Man: Can children ride the horses?

Woman: Yes, if they're over 12 years old.

Man: What other things are there to do at the farm?

Woman: Visitors milk the cows and feed the horses. They also help move the sheep to different fields. We also have lunch at the farm at 1 o'clock.

Man: Sounds lovely. And when does the farm close?

Woman: The last person leaves at half past four.

Man: Great. Thanks for the information.

Woman: You're welcome. Bye bye.

Man: Bye!

Unit 3 Listening

Assistant: Good afternoon. Can I help you?

Customer: Oh, hello. Yes, please. I'm looking for something nice for my cousin's birthday party next week. I don't have a lot of money, though!

Assistant: I understand. We're having a sale at the moment. This red skirt is lovely, but cheap – ten pounds. Do you like it?

Customer: Yes, it's very nice. But red? Have you got another colour?

Assistant: Let's see. Oh, yes. Here's a pink one.

Customer: Oh, that's my favourite colour. It matches a T-shirt I have. It also matches some new shoes I have. Yes, this skirt is perfect! Oh, just a minute. These jeans are nice too!

Assistant: Yes, and they are half-price at the moment. They're fifteen pounds.

Customer: Oh, no. Now I don't know what to buy! Hmm. No! I want the skirt!

Assistant: Great. That's ten pounds.

Customer: Here you are. Thank you very much.

Assistant: Thank you…and enjoy the party.

Unit 4 Listening

Exercise 1

Brenda: Hi, Thomas. I'm reading your review of the school play on the school website. It's a great review. You write very well!

Thomas: Thanks, Brenda. I'm glad you like it. I've got other reviews too, if you want to read them.

Exercise 2

Brenda: Hi, Thomas. I'm reading your review of the school play on the school website. It's a great review. You write very well!

Thomas: Thanks, Brenda. I'm glad you like it. I've got other reviews too, if you want to read them.

Brenda: Yes, I see that. You've got a review of the new film, *Talk of the Town*.

Thomas: Oh, right. I didn't like it, so I haven't got nice things to say about it!

Brenda: No, you haven't! My opinion of the film is it's not very good, so don't worry! But the review is good. A good review of a bad film!

Thomas: Ha, ha! Thanks for that.

Brenda: I see you've got another review here, of the film *White Nights*. I like that film, but you say it's not good. So we don't agree.

Thomas: Well, I think it's got a very sad story and it's not easy to enjoy. And it's a very long movie, really. But the actors are good.

Brenda: Hmm, well, which kind of films do you enjoy – sad films or happy films?

Thomas: If the story is good, I prefer sad films. Happy films… hmm, they're OK, but they're sometimes boring.

Brenda: I see. I don't like sad films. When I go to the cinema, I want to see something happy, not sad. But we've all got different opinions!

Thomas: Yes, I agree with that!

Unit 5 Listening

Exercise 1

Tarak: My parents and I went on a trip to Turkey last year – my big brother didn't come, so it was just us. We went for three weeks and it was amazing. We're from Egypt – that's quite close to Turkey, so we took a bus instead of a plane. The tickets were on special offer, so it wasn't very expensive. But our hotel was really nice! It had a great view of this huge river with lots of ferries on it. We had a great time visiting the sights and I took a lot of photographs with my mum's camera. I hope I go to Turkey again next year.

Sylvie: Last summer, I took a trip to Kenya. I went with my best friend Claudia and her mother Petra. It was nice and our hotel was fantastic. It had a gigantic swimming pool, but sometimes it was too noisy. Claudia and I went on a bus tour and saw lots of dangerous animals. We were on the bus, so I wasn't scared, but Claudia was. The tour guide on the bus was very funny and made people laugh with his stories about the animals. I was sad when we came back home.

Tom: My cousin Fritz and I went to South Africa last year. It was a good trip and our hotel was nice but expensive – ninety euros every night! The hotel was called 'The Great View' and it was in the centre of the city at 24 Durban Road. It was close to lots of fantastic sights. The meals were delicious at this hotel. Oh, and it had a big swimming pool on the first floor. It was very hot in South Africa, but we didn't mind – we were always in the pool!

Exercise 2

Bach: My cousin Fritz and I went to South Africa last year. It was a good trip and our hotel was nice but expensive – ninety euros every night! The hotel was called 'The Great View' and it was in the centre of the city at 24 Durban Road. It was close to lots of fantastic sights. The meals were delicious at this hotel. Oh, and it had a big swimming pool on the first floor. It was very hot in South Africa, but we didn't mind – we were always in the pool!

Unit 6 Listening

Exercise 1

Fran: Did you hear, Thomas? Paul got a python for a pet.

Thomas: Oh, really, Fran? That's cool! Pythons are interesting pets. I don't want one, but I'd like to see Paul's.

Fran: Are you kidding me? A python is a scary pet! Why can't he have a cat, like I do?

Thomas: Well, maybe he thinks cats are boring. I know I do! Those and goldfish are two very boring kinds of pets. That's why I've got Pete. He's a wonderful dog!

Exercise 2

Fran: Did you hear, Thomas? Paul got a python for a pet.

Thomas: Oh, really, Fran? That's cool! Pythons are interesting pets. I don't want one, but I'd like to see Paul's.

Fran: Are you kidding me? A python is a scary pet! Why can't he have a cat, like I do?

Thomas: Well, maybe he thinks cats are boring. I know I do! Those and goldfish are two very boring kinds of pets. That's why I've got Pete. He's a wonderful dog!

Fran: I agree about goldfish, but I think cats are terrific pets. They're easy to take care of, and fun too. The other day my cat saw a mouse and she ran to catch it. It was very funny!

Thomas: Hmm, I hate mice, so maybe that's not so bad. My friend Sasha's got a pet monkey. Can you believe that? She says it's really friendly and it doesn't cause any problems.

Fran: Oh, another strange pet! And I thought my brother Ryan's pet lizard was strange.

Thomas: A lizard for a pet? What can you do with a lizard?

Fran: He keeps it in a glass box. It's green and has got a very long tongue. He gave it a butterfly the other day for a meal. Can you believe that? A butterfly! They're so beautiful!

Thomas: Hmm. I guess for a lizard, they're tasty too!

Unit 7 Listening

Speaker 1: Hello, I'm Sophia. I'm from Egypt. Last summer, my parents and I took a trip to Portugal. We were on the plane for a long time and I was very bored. I had some magazines, but I was too tired to read them. I sat and looked at the other passengers on the plane. Then the pilot told us it was time to land. I was so excited, and a bit scared. We landed and went to get our baggage. Dad got his, Mum got hers, but mine? Mine was not there – I was not happy!

Speaker 2: My name's Vincenzo. I live in Italy. I love travelling and I take trips every year. Last year, I went to Greece. It was amazing and I had a great time visiting all the sights. I was there for two weeks. I had a plane ticket to fly home to Rome on May 5th. When I got to the airport I gave a security guard my ticket. He told me the ticket was fine but that today was the 6th! Can you believe it? I got a ticket for a ferry and got back to Rome on the 9th!

Speaker 3: Hi! My name is Fernando. I don't like travelling. I don't like buses. I don't like ferries. And I don't like planes! Planes make me feel like people feel during emergencies – unhappy and scared! Instead of travelling, I like being at home relaxing. My parents want to fly to Sydney next year, but I don't. I hope I can stay home with my grandmother. She's unhappy travelling too.

Unit 8 Listening

Monica: Tell me about your lucky escape, Trevor.

Trevor: Well, Monica, I was with my dad and we were travelling on a train through France. The train stopped at a small town that looked really interesting, so we decided to get off the train and look around. We liked the town very much and we stayed there one night. The next day, we were watching TV and there was a news report about a train crash and guess what? It was the train that we were on!

Monica: Oh, wow! You're very lucky that you decided to get off.
Trevor: Yeah, I know. Some people on the train were hurt too.
Monica: That's too bad. My family and I were in a lucky escape too. I was with my mum and sister and we were taking a boat trip from an island back to England. The weather was getting really bad and we were getting really worried. The boat was moving from side to side and I was starting to feel sick. Just then, through the window, my mum said she saw land, and I felt better when I heard that. The boat arrived 15 minutes later. I was so happy to be back on land again!
Trevor: Hmm, that sounds exciting. It's terrible you almost got sick though.
Monica: Now that it's over, yes, the boat ride was ... hmm ... interesting. But I think next time I'm only travelling by boat if the sun is shining!
Trevor: Good idea!

Unit 9 Listening

Mother: Why are you frowning, Layla? What's the matter? Did you have a bad day at school?
Layla: Oh, hi, Mum. No, school was fine ... for a Monday.
Mother: Good, so why do you look so upset?
Layla: I need to ask you about something. But I know you'll say no.
Mother: How do you know I'll say no? Ask me.
Layla: Do you know my friend, Susan Smith? I go swimming with her on Tuesdays and Thursdays.
Mother: Of course I know Susan! She lives in that gigantic house on Fair Road.
Layla: Yes, that's right. She lives at 15 Fair Road. And she's having a birthday party on Saturday, June 12th. It's her fourteenth birthday, so she's having a big party with lots of her friends.
Mother: That's nice. Is the party at her house?
Layla: No, it's at this amazing restaurant called *Lucky's*. It's near the airport, at 24 Airport Road. It's from 7pm to midnight. Can I go? Please?
Mother: But we've got tickets for a play that night. Don't you remember? You have got a short memory, Layla! It's your brother's play, at his school!
Layla: Oh, no. I forgot about that. Oh, Mum, please? I really want to go to the party.
Mother: Well, I know you really want to go, and it is a big party. And you are old enough. Yes, you can go. I want you to promise to ask Susan's dad to drive you to the restaurant and then home again after the party, though.
Layla: I promise! Thanks, Mum. Thanks for letting me go! Oh, and Mum ... can I have thirty pounds to get some new jeans or a new skirt?

Unit 10 Listening

Exercise 1

Jeffrey: Danielle, which subject do you think is better – maths or history?
Danielle: I don't know which one is better, Jeffrey. They're both important. But I think history is more interesting than maths. What do you think?
Jeffrey: I don't agree. I think maths is more interesting than history, and I also think it's more important than history. We use it a lot in life!
Danielle: I agree that maths is important, but I don't think maths is more interesting than history. Maths is quite boring, actually. It's more boring than both history and science.

Exercise 2

Jeffrey: Danielle, which subject do you think is better – maths or history?
Danielle: I don't know which one is better, Jeffrey. They're both important. But I think history is more interesting than maths. What do you think?
Jeffrey: I don't agree. I think maths is more interesting than history, and I also think it's more important than history. We use it a lot in life!
Danielle: I agree that maths is important, but I don't think maths is more interesting than history. Maths is quite boring, actually. It's more boring than both history and science.
Jeffrey: Well, science is my favourite subject, and it's a lot more exciting than maths. I agree with you that maths is more boring than science. I guess I just don't like history!
Danielle: I see. I like history, but my favourite subject is English. It's definitely more fun to study English than it is to learn about history.
Jeffrey: Well, I think it's smarter to study maths and science than English and history. Maths and science are subjects we use more often.
Danielle: OK, you study the subjects you like, and I'll study the subjects I like!
Jeffrey: I guess I can agree with that.

Unit 11 Listening

Brad: Hey, Vera. What are you thinking about?
Vera: Oh, hello, Brad. I was thinking about the future ... I was thinking about what I'm going to be when I grow up.
Brad: Wow! You're still young. Why are you thinking about that now? And you know you're going to be a famous actress! You were great in that play at the local theatre last week!
Vera: You're right, Brad. Drama school is definitely in my future! What about you? What are you going to do?
Brad: And we know that Dimitris is going to be a pilot. He's at the airport half of the time looking at the planes take off and land.
Vera: Yes, but what about you?
Brad: And Fazal, I'm sure Fazal will have a job fixing cars. He does that so well. And he's only fourteen!
Vera: Yes, yes, but what about you? What are you going ...
Brad: Then there's Julia. She said she is going to get a job developing apps for mobile phones. She talks all the time on hers, so I believe that. Kenny is going to do something like that too. I'm sure he'll work for a company that programs computers. No, no, wait! He'll work for a big

games company and play games most of the day! He's going to be very good at that. And ...

Vera: Stop, stop. Please stop! Tell me what *you* are going to do!

Brad: Me? Oh, I'm still going to be right here in Westville! I'm not going to work in a company or be famous. I'm going to be a farmer like my dad!

Unit 12 Listening

Martin: Let's talk about the six big scenes in the action movie, shall we?

Rebecca: Yes. The first scene is in the mountains, where the main character, James Z, makes his escape from Dr Wam's house. He fights Dr Wam's bad guys and runs. We see Dr Wam standing in the door, laughing and saying 'He won't go far!'

Martin: Yes, then James Z runs into a forest, where he stays for a few hours. This is the second scene.

Rebecca: Right. Dr Wam and the bad guys find him there. James Z starts to run and comes to a cliff. This is the third big scene. Dr Wam is standing in front of James Z when suddenly James Z jumps off the cliff.

Martin: Oh, that's exciting! But he's OK, right?

Rebecca: Yes. He jumps into a lake, but we don't see the lake, so we don't know what happened until later.

Martin: So we're not shooting a lake scene?

Rebecca: Right. In the fourth scene James Z is walking through open fields. He's dirty and tired, but he must keep going. Then he sees a train station and there's a train coming. He runs to catch the train.

Martin: Ah, but he doesn't know that Dr Wam is on the train.

Rebecca: Right. This is the next big scene, the fifth one. After he gets on the train, James Z sees Dr Wam and his men. The bad guys run at James Z, but James Z goes out of a window and gets on top of the train. That's where the big fight scene is.

Martin: That should be fun to shoot.

Rebecca: I know! Then the train arrives in the city. James Z and the bad guys jump from the train and they run through the city. This is the last scene. That's when James Z meets Lady Q and they fight the bad guys and win.

Martin: Oh, I thought the movie ended with a beach scene. Did that change?

Rebecca: Yes, the director said we have enough exciting places, so we'll finish shooting in the city.

Martin: OK. He's the director, so that's what we'll do!

Unit 13 Listening

Exercise 1

Enid: Oh, hi. My name is Enid Smith. And, yes, I do this telethon every year on December 14th. It's to raise money for the charity *Feed the World*. I think it's important to help poor people when you can, and it doesn't take a lot of time. The telethon is from 9am to 5pm. When you think about it, what's eight hours, one day a year? I've been here all morning, and I've spoken to more than fifty people. I've raised about three hundred euros. People are happy to give money when they know it's for charity.

Asad: Hello, I'm Asad. My school decided to have a car wash to try and collect money for the local swimming pool. It's free to use the pool and lots of students go there after school every day or on Saturdays and Sundays. But it's expensive to keep the pool open and we wanted to raise money to help. My best friend Jason and I have washed four cars in one hour. We make five euros for every car, so that means we've made twenty euros!

Angela: My name's Angela. Last month, I saw a website about children in Africa that want to go to school, but can't because the place where they live is so poor. The website said there was a charity that was raising money to build a school for these children. I told my cousin Antonio and my friend Julia about it and we decided to help. Every day after school we walk dogs! There are people who have got dogs, but who don't always have the time to take them out, so we do it for them. We make seven euros for every hour we walk the dogs. We've raised more than 400 euros for the school in Africa!

Exercise 2

Enid: Oh, hi. My name is Enid Smith. And, yes, I do this telethon every year on December 14th. It's to raise money for the charity *Feed the World*. I think it's important to help poor people when you can, and it doesn't take a lot of time. The telethon is from 9am to 5pm. When you think about it, what's eight hours, one day a year? I've been here all morning, and I've spoken to more than fifty people. I've raised about three hundred euros. People are happy to give money when they know it's for charity.

Unit 14 Listening

Angie: Is it easy to get to your new school, Martin?

Martin: Yes, it's much easier than getting to the old school, Angie. And it's only 20 minutes away.

Angie: I've heard of the school, but I don't know where it is. How do you get there from your house?

Martin: Well, my dad takes me to school, but first you go straight down East Road. That's my street. Then when you get to the first traffic lights, you turn left. That's Market Street.

Angie: I know where Market Street is. My favourite clothes shop is on that street.

Martin: Yes, we go past that clothes shop every day. So, you go down Market Street for about 10 minutes. Then, when you get to the police station, you turn right onto Crabtree Road. You go straight ahead for a bit, and when you get to the next crossroads, you're there!

Angie: That sounds easy.

Martin: It's quite easy, but we got lost on the first day! My dad turned left onto Crabtree Road and the road ended. We had to turn round! But I wasn't late for class, which was good.

Angie: Well, now you know the way, you'll never get lost again!

Martin: Right!